The Latest
Cast Iron
Cookbook

1200 Days Cast Iron Skillet & Dutch Oven Recipes for Beginners and Advanced Users

Joyce Powell

Table of Contents

You will love Cast Iron Cookware. It's strong, reliable, and a great addition to your kitchen. Chefs have been cooking with cast iron for hundreds of years and we want to continue that tradition!

"Cast Iron" name is not new to us. We all know it's a soft metal that can be molded into many useful products. Can you know that cast iron is also used in pots? Yes, you can have cast iron pots and pans for cooking. This amazing pan allows you to sear, bake, cook, sauté your food with restaurant quality perfection. It gives a unique texture and taste to the food and everyone will enjoy it.

This guide will help you to know all about cast iron and what you can cook in it with perfection.

A type of kitchen utensil made of a soft, heavy metal material known as cast iron, which is an excellent material for cooking food. Cast Iron Cookware absorbs heat well, retains heat, and distributes it evenly along the length and width of the stove. The Cast Iron Cookware can be treated with a manufacturer's paint, such as porcelain enamel, or it can be uncoated. Uncoated cast iron requires seasoning with oil for use in making a non-stick surface, while coated cast iron usually does not require seasoning.

This guide will help you to know all about Cast Iron Cookware and what you can cook in it with perfection.

You probably know what Iron looks like. Those dark, heavy pots and pans such as something you see in camping. And yes they are good for campsite limit, but that's all not everything. Cast Iron Cookware is made by melting iron and steel. This magus tipple is then shaped in the form of a skillet, griddle, or Dutch oven. At cooling mold is opened to shining new cook tools. Cast Iron is cooked for centuries. The first documented use was in 220 A.D.in ancient China. In the past several hundred years streamlined manufacturing of hard pots and pans are ubiquitous in the world.

How to Season Cast Iron Cookware

The best way to feel good is to season your Cast Iron Cookware and cook with it. Make your pot "cooking" and create a way to use it anytime. Every time you heat Cast Iron Cookware add oil to it, it polymerizes, adding a new thin layer of non-stick coating to your skillet or Dutch oven. This layer is done until you have a perfect Cast Iron Cookware. It makes cooking a dream come true! The Ideal seasoning of the Cast Iron Cookware is performed in the set temperatures allow for polymerization to occur oil bonding with iron, but not for the oil to smoke and ultimately turn into burnt carbon. A slow and steady cook time allows even heating, and the oil to heat with it.

The following steps will help you to season your Cast Iron Cookware effectively and cooking-worthy.

1. Remove cast iron packaging and wipe off any dirt or debris.
2. Preheat the oven to 300 degrees F.
3. Bring cooking oil. Sunflower, grape seed, or other high smoke oils are recommended.
4. Oil the inside surface of the Cast Iron Cookware. Pour about a teaspoon at a time and pull up with a paper towel properly. Make sure to cover the walls of the pan with oil also.
5. The Cast Iron Cookware has a porous surface. You need to rub little oil on the surface. Do this several times until the Cast Iron Cookware is well greased but not dripping.
6. Put the Cast Iron Cookware in the oven for 10 minutes. Remove the cast iron and wipe off excess oil on the surface Cast Iron Cookware is hot, so remove carefully!
7. Preheat the oven to 400 degrees F.
8. Place the pot back in the oven and cook for an hour and do not open the oven until time out.
9. Remove it from the oven and let it cool before cooking.

Your Cast Iron Cookware is fully prepared for cooking. You can cook whatever you want.

Seasoning Your Cookware

The following steps are helpful for the proper seasoning of the Cast Iron Cookware.

Step 1: Wash and Dry Your Pan
Wash your new cast iron cookware before starting to season. Give the pan a good scrub with warm, soapy water, and then dry it thoroughly. Even after towel-drying, some surface moisture may remain, so put the pan on a stovetop flame for a minute or two to drive off any lingering water.

Step 2: Rub It All Over with Oil and Buff Well
Now that your pan is clean and dry, rub it all over, inside and out including the handle with cooking oil. You can use vegetables, canola, and corn oil, for seasoning pans. Rub the oil all over, and then buff it so thoroughly that the pan no longer looks even the slightest bit greasy.

Step 3: Heat It in the Oven
Put the oiled pan in a preheated 450°F oven, and leave it there for 30 minutes. It may get a little smoky, so keep your kitchen well ventilated.

Step 4: Repeat 3 to 4 Times
When the half-hour is up, take the pan out. Now rub it once more all over with the oil, buffing it out as before. Then put it back in the oven for another 30 minutes. All in all, you'll want to do this oiling-and-heating process three to four times, to set down a good initial layer of your seasoning.

Once you're done, just let the pan cool down. It's now ready for cooking.

Prepping Pre-Seasoned Cookware

Some people feel that cast iron requires a lot of care and should follow the above procedures to keep the pan in good working order. Not really! Now all you need is a Cast Iron Cookware. Every time you cook with oil, you'll end up adding seasoning. Once the seasonings are well established, the Cast Iron Cookware can be used without worry for acidic foods like tomatoes and sauces.

Need help thinking about how? Try the fried chicken, roast, fried eggs, and sautéed vegetables. Frying bread, such as cornbread, will also help season the pan.

And that's the point here. A good old cast iron skillet is well used. Use it to spend more time in the kitchen and less time in online forums Arguing about it is a good first step.

Re-Seasoning Your Cookware

For re-season you Cast Iron Cookware, all you will need is some steel wool, paper towels or rags, your oven, and some cooking oil.

1. Clean it thoroughly with warm, soapy water.
2. Next, you'll want to break out the steel wool. Scrub it to get off the grime. Scrub until clean.

3. Next, grab some paper towels or rags and keep rubbing.
4. Once you're down past all the rust and carbon, you're ready to treat that old skillet the same way you'd treat a new one.
5. Preheat your oven to 350°F, break out some paper towels and a little vegetable oil, and you're ready to go.
6. Cover the entire surface with a thin coating of oil.
7. Put the pan upside-down in the oven and bake it for an hour.
8. Remove it from the oven, and once it's cool enough to handle, rub a paper towel or rag across the surface.
9. Once the towel comes clean, you have a seasoned surface.

Cleaning Cast Iron

The use of cast iron helps to reduce water consumption. In most cases, you can use a paper towel or specialty rag to wipe excess oil and debris from your frying pan or Dutch pan. Oil is meant to control room temperature, so a small amount in a frying pan or Dutch oven won't cause mold or other problems.

If you need to wash deeper or dispose of food particles, follow the instructions below.

1. Scrub the cast iron with a brush, stainless steel cleaning net, or salt brush in warm water.
2. Let the cast iron pan dry for a few minutes on the stove or hot plate. Heat until the water evaporates, but the cast iron begins to smoke. This process reduces the risk of rust by drying the cast iron.
3. When the cast iron cools, lightly coat the cast iron skillet with cooking oil such as olive or avocado to maintain seasoning.
4. Use a paper towel or dedicated rags for seasoning oil to the pan.
5. For long-term storage, cover the cast iron pot with a towel to keep dust out from the oiled surface.

Cast Iron Storage

Professional chefs must have cast iron utensils in their kitchen: frying pan, sauté pan, griddle, or wok. Cast iron comes in fantastic shapes and sizes to fit everything you need for cooking. But cast iron cookware is heavy and bulky, so you have to think about where to store it. Proper storage of cast iron will keep your cookware on top for your next cooking event. It should prevent corrosion and prolong life exponentially!

Exactly where to store your cast iron cookware depends on your kitchen layout, the space available, and the number of cooking utensils you need to secure. Here are a few tips.

1. Store Cast Iron Cookware in a cool, dry place.
2. Store Cast Iron Cookware only when clean and dry. This will protect the pan from rusting.
3. Protect the Cast Iron Cookware by wrapping it in a paper towel.

Dos and Don'ts

A well-seasoned Cast Iron Cookware takes time, patience, and care. However, that doesn't mean you have to cuddle it like your baby or put it to bed every night. Cast Iron Cookware is a tough, versatile material that performs well at high temperatures, even at high temperatures, but requires care.

Do's
• Always Use dish soap for cleaning your Cast Iron Cookware. If found tough food that is not clear with soap. try gentle scrubbing with oil, salt, and paper towel gently until the pot is clean.
• Wash the Cast Iron Cookware properly and rub the Cast Iron Cookware with oil before storing and cover it in a towel to avoid dust and dirt.
• Season your pans twice a year for effective cooking.
• Use your pan on the grill for cooking as well as on the oven for baking. It will enhance the efficiency of the pot.

Don'ts
• Don't put your cookware away wet. It is harmful and causes rust on the metal.
• Don't put your Cast Iron Cookware in the dishwasher as it is harsh for the Cast Iron Cookware surface.
• Don't soak your Cast Iron Cookware in the sink for long in the water.
• Never store the food in this Cast Iron Cookware.
• Never use metal or sharp utensils to scrub stuck food.

Baked Butter Cornbread

Prep Time: 10 minutes
Cook Time: 25 minutes
Serves: 8
Ingredients:
- 1 egg
- 1 cup cheddar cheese, grated
- 1 cup corn kernel
- ¼ cup olive oil
- 1 cup buttermilk
- 4 teaspoons baking powder
- ¼ cup sugar
- 1 cup flour
- 1 cup cornmeal
- ¼ cup butter
- ½ teaspoon salt

Preparation:
1. Preheat the oven to 425°F.
2. Mix the flour, baking powder, sugar, cornmeal, and salt in a bowl.
3. Add the oil, milk, and egg and stir until well combined.
4. Add the grated cheese and corn kernels and fold well.
5. Melt the butter in a cast-iron skillet over medium heat.
6. Pour the batter into the hot skillet and spread evenly.
7. Place the skillet in the preheated oven and bake for 25 minutes.

Serving Suggestion: Slice and serve.
Variation Tip: You can use regular milk instead of buttermilk.

Nutritional Information Per Serving:
Calories 341 | Fat 18.4g | Sodium 321mg | Carbs 38.1g | Fiber 2.5g | Sugar 8.5g | Protein 9g

Fluffy Milk Cornbread

Prep Time: 15 minutes
Cook Time: 25 minutes
Serves: 8
Ingredients:
- 1 cup flour
- 1 cup cornmeal
- ⅔ cup white sugar
- 1 tablespoon baking powder
- 1 cup whole milk
- 1 teaspoon salt
- 1 egg
- ⅓ cup vegetable oil

Preparation:
1. Preheat the oven to 400°F and lightly grease an 8-inch cast-iron wok.
2. Add the cornmeal, flour, sugar, baking powder, and salt to a large bowl and mix well.
3. Add the egg, milk, and oil to another bowl and beat until well combined.
4. Add the flour mixture and mix until just combined.
5. Place the mixture into the prepared wok.
6. Bake for about 20–25 minutes in the preheated oven or until a toothpick inserted in the center of the mixture comes out clean.
7. Remove the wok from the oven and place it onto a wire rack to cool for at least 10 minutes.
8. Carefully invert the bread onto a platter.
9. Cut the bread into the desired sized slices with a sharp knife and serve warm.

Serving Suggestions: Serve with the garnishing of fresh mint.
Variation Tip: Maple syrup can be replaced with honey.

Nutritional Information per Serving:
Calories: 293|Fat: 12.4g|Sat Fat: 3.3g|Carbohydrates: 42.8g|Fiber: 1.6g|Sugar: 18.1g|Protein: 4.6g

Garlic Cheese Waffles

Prep Time: 10 minutes
Cook Time: 6 minutes
Serves: 2
Ingredients:
- 2 organic eggs, beaten
- ½ cup parmesan cheese, shredded
- 1 teaspoon onion powder
- 1 tablespoon chives, minced
- 1 cup cauliflower
- 1 cup mozzarella cheese, shredded
- ½ teaspoon ground black pepper
- 1 teaspoon garlic powder

Preparation:
1. Combine all the ingredients in a bowl.
2. Grease a cast iron waffle maker and heat it.
3. Trickle half of the mixture into the waffle iron and cook until golden brown.
4. Repeat with the remaining mixture and serve.
Serving Suggestions: Serve with the garnishing of scallions.
Variation Tip: You can also use cheddar cheese in these waffles.
Nutritional Information per Serving:
Calories: 171|Fat: 10g|Sat Fat: 4.9g|Carbohydrates: 6.4g|Fiber: 1.6g|Sugar: 2.3g|Protein: 15.5g

Eggs in Bell Pepper

Prep Time: 5 minutes
Cook Time: 6 minutes
Serves: 2
Ingredients:
- 4 eggs
- 2 tablespoons fresh parsley, chopped
- 1 green bell pepper, cut into 4 (¼-inch) rings and seeded
- Salt and black pepper, as required
Preparation:
1. Heat a large, lightly greased cast-iron wok over medium heat.

2. Place the bell pepper rings in the wok and cook for about 2 minutes.
3. Flip the rings and then crack an egg in the middle of each.
4. Sprinkle each egg with salt and black pepper and cook for about 4 minutes until the desired doneness of the eggs.
Serving Suggestion: Serve with the garnishing of parsley and dill.
Variation Tip: You can also use red and yellow bell peppers.
Nutritional Information per Serving:
Calories: 146|Fat: 8.9g|Sat Fat: 3.1g|Carbohydrates: 5.4g|Fiber: 0.9g|Sugar: 3.7g|Protein: 11.8g

Tater Tot Sausage Pizza

Prep Time: 10 minutes
Cook Time: 25 minutes
Serves: 8
Ingredients:
- 6 eggs, lightly beaten
- ¾ cup sausage, cooked and crumbled
- ¾ cup bacon, cooked and crumbled
- 2 cups cheddar cheese, shredded
- ½ tablespoon olive oil
- 30 ounces' tater tots
- Pepper
- Salt

Preparation:
1. Preheat the oven to 425°F.
2. Spray a 12-inch cast-iron skillet with cooking spray.
3. Arrange the tater tots into the greased skillet and bake them in the oven for 15 minutes.
4. Meanwhile, heat the oil in a pan over medium heat.
5. Add the eggs and season them with salt and pepper; cook until just set.
6. Remove the tater tots from the oven and press down on them using a spatula. Top them with 1 cup of cheddar cheese.
7. Then add the eggs, cooked sausage, remaining cheese, and sprinkle with bacon.
8. Bake in the oven for 10 minutes more.
Serving Suggestion: Slice and serve.
Variation Tip: You can substitute cheddar cheese with mozzarella cheese.
Nutritional Information Per Serving:
Calories 444 | Fat 28.4g | Sodium 1045mg | Carbs 30.3g | Fiber 2.7g | Sugar 0.7g | Protein 18.3g

Skillet-Fried Sweet Potatoes

Prep Time: 10 minutes
Cook Time: 12 minutes
Serves: 4
Ingredients:
• 1½ pounds sweet potatoes, peeled and cut into ½-inch cubes
• ¼ teaspoon nutmeg
• ½ teaspoon cinnamon
• 2 teaspoons fresh thyme
• 2 tablespoons olive oil
• Pepper
• Salt
Preparation:
1. Heat the oil in a 12-inch cast-iron skillet over medium heat.
2. Add the sweet potato cubes and seasonings to the skillet and sauté until the sweet potato is fork-tender.
Serving Suggestion: Garnish with fresh chopped parsley and serve.
Variation Tip: Add your choice of seasonings.
Nutritional Information Per Serving:
Calories 264 | Fat 7.4g | Sodium 54mg | Carbs 48.1g | Fiber 7.4g | Sugar 0.9g | Protein 2.7g

Potato Pancake

Prep Time: 10 minutes
Cook Time: 10 minutes
Serves: 4
Ingredients:
• 4 eggs, lightly beaten
• 4 bacon slices, cooked and chopped
• ¾ cup cheddar cheese, shredded
• 1 tablespoon olive oil
• ½ bag frozen shredded hash brown potatoes

• Pepper
• Salt
Preparation:
1. Preheat the oven to 350°F.
2. Heat the oil in a cast-iron skillet over medium heat.
3. Add the potatoes to the skillet, cook until lightly browned, and season with salt and pepper.
4. Add ½ cup of shredded cheese, eggs, bacon, and remaining cheese and bake in the preheated oven for 10 minutes.
Serving Suggestion: Garnish with sliced scallions and serve.
Variation Tip: Add your choice of seasonings.
Nutritional Information Per Serving:
Calories 297 | Fat 23.7g | Sodium 708mg | Carbs 2.8g | Fiber 0.3g | Sugar 0.5g | Protein 18g

Scrambled Potatoes with Mushrooms

Prep Time: 10 minutes
Cook Time: 15 minutes
Serves: 8
Ingredients:
• 24 ounces' potatoes, cut into bite-size pieces
• ¼ cup pre-cooked ham, diced
• ½ teaspoon dried thyme
• ½ teaspoon dried rosemary
• 2 tablespoons olive oil
• ½ onion, chopped
• 6 ounces' mushrooms, sliced
• Pepper
• Salt
Preparation:
1. Mix the potatoes, oil, thyme, rosemary, onions, pepper, and salt in a mixing bowl.
2. Add the potatoes to a cast-iron skillet and cook over medium heat for 10 minutes.
3. Add the mushrooms and ham and cook for 3–5 minutes.
Serving Suggestion: Garnish with freshly chopped parsley and serve.
Variation Tip: Add your choice of seasonings.
Nutritional Information Per Serving:
Calories 99 | Fat 3.8g | Sodium 37mg | Carbs 14.8g | Fiber 2.5g | Sugar 1.6g | Protein 2.6g

Vanilla Dates and Quinoa

Prep Time: 10 minutes
Cook Time: 15 minutes
Serves: 2
Ingredients:
- ½ cup red quinoa, dried
- ⅛ teaspoon vanilla extract
- 1 date, pitted and finely chopped
- 1 cup unsweetened almond milk
- ¼ cup fresh strawberries, hulled and sliced
- ⅛ teaspoon ground cinnamon

Preparation:
1. Mix the quinoa, almond milk, cinnamon, and vanilla in a cast-iron skillet over low heat.
2. Cook for about 15 minutes while stirring occasionally.
3. Garnish with strawberries and serve.

Serving Suggestions: Top with chopped almonds and blueberries.
Variation Tip: You can also use coconut milk instead of almond milk.
Nutritional Information per Serving:
Calories: 455|Fat: 31.2g|Sat Fat: 25.4g|Carbohydrates: 41.3g|Fiber: 6.4g|Sugar: 10.6g|Protein: 9g

Turkey and Veggies Hash

Prep Time: 10 minutes
Cook Time: 14 minutes
Serves: 2
Ingredients:
- ½ small onion, chopped
- ½ teaspoon dried thyme, crushed
- 1 tablespoon butter

- ¼ cup heavy cream
- ½ pound turkey meat, cooked and chopped
- ½ cup cauliflower florets, boiled
- Salt and black pepper, to taste

Preparation:
1. Blend the cauliflower florets in a chopper and keep them aside.
2. Put the butter and onions in a cast-iron skillet and sauté for about 3 minutes.
3. Add the chopped cauliflower and sauté for about 3 more minutes.
4. Add the turkey and cook for about 6 minutes.
5. Stir in the heavy cream and cook for about 2 minutes, stirring constantly.
6. Dish out to serve.

Serving Suggestions: Serve sprinkled with black pepper.
Variation Tip: You can also use cooked chicken meat.
Nutritional Information per Serving:
Calories: 310|Fat: 17.1g|Sat Fat: 9g|Carbohydrates: 3.6g|Fiber: 1.1g|Sugar: 1.4g|Protein: 34.3g

Scrambled Tomato and Pepper

Prep Time: 15 minutes
Cook Time: 6 minutes
Serves: 2
Ingredients:
- 2 tablespoons scallions, thinly sliced
- 3 tablespoons butter
- 4 large organic eggs
- ¼ cup heavy cream
- 1 small tomato, chopped
- 1 Serrano chili pepper
- 2 tablespoons cilantro, finely chopped
- Salt and black pepper, to taste

Preparation:
1. Combine the cream, eggs, cilantro, salt, and black pepper in a medium bowl.
2. Put the butter, tomatoes, and Serrano pepper in a cast-iron skillet on medium heat and sauté for about 2 minutes.
3. Add the egg mixture to the skillet and cook for about 4 minutes, continuously stirring.

Serving Suggestions: Garnish with scallions and serve immediately.
Variation Tip: You can also use more chilies.
Nutritional Information per Serving:
Calories: 359|Fat: 32.9g|Sat Fat: 17.5g|Carbohydrates: 3.7g|Fiber: 0.9g|Sugar: 2.3g|Protein: 13.7g

Baked Cheese Bread

Prep Time: 10 minutes
Cook Time: 25 minutes
Serves: 6
Ingredients:
• 2 cups cheddar cheese, shredded
• 3 tablespoons butter, melted
• 12 ounces' beer
• 4 teaspoons baking powder
• 2 tablespoons sugar
• 1½ teaspoons garlic powder
• 1½ tablespoons dried parsley
• 2½ cups all-purpose flour
• 2 tablespoons olive oil
• 1 teaspoon salt
Preparation:
1. Add the olive oil to a 10-inch cast-iron skillet.
2. Place the skillet in the oven and preheat it to 450°F.
3. Mix the flour, garlic powder, baking powder, sugar, parsley, and salt in a mixing bowl. Add the cheese and beer and mix until well combined.
4. Once the oven is preheated, remove the skillet. Spread the flour mixture into the skillet.
5. Pour the melted butter on top of the flour mixture.
6. Bake in the preheated oven for 25 minutes.
Serving Suggestion: Let the bread cool for 10 minutes, then slice and serve.
Variation Tip: You can substitute cheddar cheese for any other cheese you like.
Nutritional Information Per Serving:
Calories 478 | Fat 23.6g | Sodium 711mg | Carbs 52g | Fiber 2.7g | Sugar 9g | Protein 15.9g

Cheesy Omelet

Prep Time: 10 minutes
Cook Time: 30 minutes
Serves: 6
Ingredients:
• 5 eggs
• 4 egg whites
• ½ cup cheddar cheese, shredded
• ½ cup ham, diced
• ½ cup bell pepper, diced
• ½ cup onion, diced
• 1½ teaspoons olive oil
• ¼ cup milk
• Pepper
• Salt
Preparation:
1. Preheat the oven to 400°F.
2. Whisk the eggs with the milk, pepper, and salt in a mixing bowl and set aside.
3. Heat the oil in a 10-inch cast-iron skillet over medium-high heat.
4. Add the bell peppers and onion to the skillet and sauté for 5 minutes, then season with salt and pepper.
5. Add the ham and cook for another minute.
6. Add the egg mixture, then sprinkle with the shredded cheese.
7. Place the skillet into the preheated oven and bake for 25 minutes or until the omelet is set.
Serving Suggestion: Slice and serve.
Variation Tip: You can also add 1 teaspoon of hot sauce to the egg mixture.
Nutritional Information Per Serving:
Calories 142 | Fat 9.2g | Sodium 311mg | Carbs 3.1g | Fiber 0.5g | Sugar 1.9g | Protein 11.8g

Vanilla Oatmeal

Prep Time: 10 minutes
Cook Time: 45 minutes
Serves: 8
Ingredients:
• 2 eggs
• ¾ cup walnuts
• ¾ cup hazelnuts
• ⅓ cup maple syrup
• 1 teaspoon vanilla
• 1½ cups unsweetened almond milk
• ¾ teaspoon baking powder
• ¾ teaspoon cinnamon
• 1½ cups rolled oats
• 4 cups cherries, pitted
• ½ teaspoon salt
Preparation:

1. Preheat the oven to 350°F.
2. Spray a cast-iron skillet with cooking spray.
3. Spread the cherries into the bottom of the skillet and set it aside.
4. Mix the oats, baking powder, cinnamon, and salt in a mixing bowl.
5. In a separate bowl, whisk the eggs with the maple syrup, vanilla, and milk until well combined.
6. Add the egg mixture to the oat mixture and stir well to combine.
7. Pour the mixture over the cherries in the skillet. Top with the walnuts and hazelnuts.
8. Bake in the preheated oven for 45 minutes.
Serving Suggestion: Let it cool for 5 minutes, then cut into pieces and serve.
Variation Tip: You can add your choice of nuts.
Nutritional Information Per Serving:
Calories 277 | Fat 14g | Sodium 206mg | Carbs 32.8g | Fiber 3.6g | Sugar 8.6g | Protein 7.6g

Green Apple Omelet

Prep Time: 10 minutes
Cook Time: 9 minutes
Serves: 1
Ingredients:
• ½ large green apple, cored and sliced thinly
• 2 teaspoons coconut oil, divided
• ¼ teaspoon ground cinnamon
• 2 large eggs
• Pinch of salt
• ⅛ teaspoon ground nutmeg
• ⅛ teaspoon vanilla extract
Preparation:
1. In a cast-iron frying pan, melt 1 teaspoon of coconut oil over medium-low heat and cook the apple slices with nutmeg and cinnamon for about 5 minutes, flipping once halfway through.
2. Meanwhile, add the eggs, vanilla, and salt to a bowl and beat until fluffy.
3. Add the remaining oil to the pan and let it heat up.
4. Place the egg mixture evenly over the apple slices and cook for about 4 minutes or until the desired doneness of the egg.
5. Carefully turn the pan over a serving plate and immediately fold the omelet.

6. Serve hot.
Serving Suggestions: Serve with toasted bread slices.
Variation Tip: You can also use olive oil.
Nutritional Information per Serving:
Calories: 284|Fat: 19.3g|Sat Fat: 5.9g|Carbohydrates: 16.9g|Fiber: 3.1g|Sugar: 12.5g|Protein: 12.9g

Chicken Zucchini Pancakes with Scallion

Prep Time: 15 minutes
Cook Time: 32 minutes
Serves: 4
Ingredients:
• 4 cups zucchini, shredded
• Salt, as required
• ¼ cup scallion, chopped finely
• ¼ cup coconut flour
• 2 tablespoons olive oil
• ¼ cup cooked chicken, shredded
• 1 egg, beaten
• Ground black pepper, as required
Preparation:
1. Put the zucchini in a colander and sprinkle with salt.
2. Leave it for about 10 minutes, then squeeze the zucchini well.
3. Add the zucchini and remaining ingredients to a bowl and mix until well combined.
4. In a large-sized cast-iron wok, heat the oil over medium heat.
5. Add ¼ cup of the zucchini mixture and cook for about 3–4 minutes per side.
6. Repeat with the remaining mixture and serve warm.
Serving Suggestions: Serve with your choice of dip.
Variation Tip: You can also use almond flour.
Nutritional Information per Serving:
Calories: 113|Fat: 8.7g|Sat Fat: 2.9g|Carbohydrates: 4.9g|Fiber: 1.7g|Sugar: 2.2g|Protein: 5.5g

Butter Chicken Asparagus Frittata

Prep Time: 15 minutes
Cook Time: 12 minutes
Serves: 4
Ingredients:
• ⅓ cup parmesan cheese, grated
• ½ cup cooked chicken, chopped
• 6 eggs, beaten lightly
• 1 teaspoon unsalted butter
• 1 tablespoon fresh parsley, chopped
• Salt and black pepper, to taste
• ½ cup boiled asparagus, chopped
Preparation:
1. Preheat the broiler of your oven.
2. Add the cheese, eggs, salt, and black pepper to a bowl and beat until well combined.
3. In a large-sized cast-iron wok, melt the butter over medium-high heat and cook the chicken and asparagus for about 2–3 minutes.
4. Add the egg mixture and stir to combine.
5. Cook for about 5 minutes.
6. Remove the wok from the heat and sprinkle the mixture with the parsley.
7. Put the wok under the broiler and broil for about 4 minutes.
8. Cut into desired-sized wedges and serve immediately.
Serving Suggestion: Serve with a topping of tomato sauce.
Variation Tip: Add in seasonings of your choice.
Nutritional Information per Serving:
Calories: 157|Fat: 1.2g|Sat Fat: 0.1g|Carbohydrates: 1.2g|Fiber: 0.4g|Sugar: 0.8g|Protein: 16.5g

Scalloped Potatoes

Prep Time: 10 minutes
Cook Time: 1 hour 15 minutes

Serves: 6
Ingredients:
• 6 medium potatoes, peeled and thinly sliced
• 1 teaspoon garlic, minced
• 1½ cups Gruyere cheese, shredded
• 1½ cups milk
• 3 tablespoons all-purpose flour
• 3 tablespoons butter
• Pepper
• Salt
Preparation:
1. Preheat the oven to 400°F.
2. Melt the butter in a 9-inch cast-iron skillet over medium heat.
3. Once the butter is melted, turn the heat to low, add the flour, and stir for 30 seconds.
4. Add the garlic, milk, pepper, and salt and stir until smooth. Remove the skillet from the heat and pour the milk mixture into the mixing bowl.
5. Arrange the potato slices into the same skillet in an overlapping spiral pattern and season with salt and pepper.
6. Sprinkle half the shredded cheese over the potatoes.
7. Pour the milk mixture over the potatoes, then sprinkle with the remaining cheese.
8. Cover with foil and bake in the preheated oven for 60 minutes.
9. Remove the foil and bake for 5–10 minutes more.
Serving Suggestion: Let it cool for 10 minutes, then serve.
Variation Tip: You can substitute Gruyere cheese with mozzarella, cheddar, or any other cheese you prefer.
Nutritional Information Per Serving:
Calories 355 | Fat 16g | Sodium 200mg | Carbs 39.7g | Fiber 5.2g | Sugar 5.3g | Protein 14.1g

Sausage and Vegetable Hash

Prep Time: 10 minutes
Cook Time: 25 minutes
Serves: 8
Ingredients:
• 12 eggs, lightly beaten
• 1 cup cheddar cheese, shredded
• ¼ cup green pepper, chopped
• ¼ cup onion, chopped
• 7 ounces' breakfast sausage, cooked and cut into ½-inch pieces
• 40 ounces shredded hash brown potatoes
• ¼ cup butter, cubed
• Pepper
• Salt
Preparation:

1. Melt the butter in a 12-inch cast-iron skillet over medium heat.
2. Add the potatoes, green pepper, onion, and sausage and cook over medium heat for 15–20 minutes or until the potatoes are lightly browned.
3. Push the mixture to the sides of the skillet.
4. Pour the eggs into the center of the skillet. Stir and cook over medium heat until the eggs are set, then season with salt and pepper.
5. Turn the heat to low and stir the eggs into the sausage and potato mixture. Top with the shredded cheddar cheese, cover, and cook until the cheese is melted.
Serving Suggestion: Stir well and serve warm.
Variation Tip: Add your choice of seasonings.
Nutritional Information Per Serving:
Calories 664 | Fat 41.8g | Sodium 911mg | Carbs 50.9g | Fiber 4.7g | Sugar 2.9g | Protein 21g

Tasty Oat Pancakes

Prep Time: 15 minutes
Cook Time: 24 minutes
Serves: 6
Ingredients:
• 1 cup old-fashioned oats
• ½ cup all-purpose flour
• 2 tablespoons flaxseeds
• Salt, as required
• 2 large eggs
• 2 tablespoons extra-virgin olive oil
• 1 teaspoon baking soda
• 2 tablespoons agave nectar
• 2 cups plain Greek yogurt
Preparation:
1. Put the flour, oats, flaxseeds, baking soda, and salt in a blender and pulse until well combined.
2. Transfer the mixture into a large-sized bowl
3. Add the remaining ingredients except the oil and mix until well combined.
4. Keep aside for about 20 minutes before cooking.
5. Heat a large-sized cast-iron wok over medium heat and grease with a little oil.

6. Add ¼ cup of the mixture and cook for about 2 minutes or until the bottom becomes golden brown.
7. Carefully flip it over and cook for about 2 minutes more.
8. Repeat with the remaining mixture and serve warm.
Serving Suggestions: Serve drizzled with honey and butter.
Variation Tip: You can also use almond flour for a gluten-free diet.
Nutritional Information per Serving:
Calories: 239|Fat: 9g|Sat Fat: 1.5g|Carbohydrates: 26.4g|Fiber: 2.2g|Sugar: 2.7g|Protein: 13g

Wok-Fried Onion with Cheddar

Prep Time: 10 minutes
Cook Time: 8 minutes
Serves: 6
Ingredients:
• 1 small yellow onion, chopped finely
• 2 tablespoons olive oil
• 12 large eggs, beaten lightly
• 4 ounces' cheddar cheese, shredded
• Salt and black pepper, as required
Preparation:
1. Heat the oil over medium heat in a large-sized cast-iron wok and sauté the onion for about 4–5 minutes.
2. Add the eggs, salt, and black pepper and cook for about 3 minutes, stirring continuously.
3. Remove the pan from the heat and immediately stir in the cheese.
4. Serve immediately.
Serving Suggestion: Serve with buttered toast.
Variation Tip: You can also add in some mozzarella cheese.
Nutritional Information per Serving:
Calories: 264|Fat: 20.4g|Sat Fat: 5.6g|Carbohydrates: 2.1g|Fiber: 0.3g|Sugar: 1.4g|Protein: 17.4g

Fried Eggs and Bacon

Prep Time: 10 minutes
Cook Time: 25 minutes
Serves: 4
Ingredients:
- 8 ounces thick-cut bacon
- 1 tablespoon salted butter
- 4 eggs
- Pinch of sea salt

Preparation:
1. Arrange the bacon in your cast-iron pan, ensuring the pieces don't touch.
2. Heat the pan over medium-low heat and cook the bacon until it crisps around the edges, about 10 minutes.
3. Flip the bacon and increase the heat to medium-high.
4. Allow the pan to cool slightly and drain off the grease, leaving a residual layer.
5. Put the pan over medium heat and melt the butter.
6. Crack the eggs into the pan so that they're evenly spaced. Sprinkle the yolks with salt.
7. When the rim of the yolk is cooked through (after about 5 minutes), flip the egg and cook for 1 minute before serving.

Serving Suggestion: Garnish with chives.
Variation Tip: Add a sprinkle of paprika while serving for added flavor.
Nutritional Information per Serving:
Calories 266 | Fat 24.1g | Sodium 422mg | Carbs 0.8g | Fiber 0g | Sugar 0.3g | Protein 10.9g

Simple Caprese Eggs

Prep Time: 10 minutes
Cook Time: 20 minutes
Serves: 4
Ingredients:
- 3 tomatoes, chopped
- ½ cup onion, chopped
- 4 eggs
- 2 tablespoons olive oil
- ½ teaspoon salt
- 4 teaspoons fresh oregano
- 4 teaspoons fresh chives
- 4 teaspoons fresh basil
- ½ teaspoon black pepper
- ½ cup mozzarella cheese

Preparation:
1. Place a 10-inch cast-iron skillet onto the stove, and set to medium heat. Pour in the oil and heat.
2. Once the oil is hot, sauté the onion until tender and almost translucent, between 3 to 5 minutes.
3. Fold in the tomatoes and season with salt and pepper.
4. Cook for about 5 minutes, or until the tomatoes are soft. Stir frequently while cooking.
5. Once the tomatoes are soft, make an indentation in the tomato mixture using a wooden spoon. Repeat until you have four wells or indentations in the tomatoes. Carefully crack an egg into each well.
6. Place a lid on the cast iron skillet, and continue to cook until the whites are firm and the yolks are still soft.
7. Shred the mozzarella cheese.
8. Once the eggs are the desired consistency, sprinkle the dish with the shredded cheese.
9. Return the lid to the skillet, and cook for an additional minute.
10. Toss together the oregano, basil, and chives.
11. Remove from the heat, and serve.

Serving Suggestion: Serve on its own or with toast and sprinkle the herbs on top.
Variation Tip: Switch up mozzarella cheese with feta or goat's cheese.
Nutritional Information per Serving:
Calories 161 | Fat 12.4g | Sodium 379mg | Carbs 6.6g | Fiber 2.2g | Sugar 3.5g | Protein 7.8g

Sausage and Potato Hash

Prep Time: 10 minutes
Cook Time: 30 minutes
Serves: 4
Ingredients:
- 8 ounces' chorizo sausage, coarsely chopped
- 2 tablespoons salted butter
- 1 white onion, chopped
- 2 garlic cloves, minced
- 2 cups potatoes, shredded (1 to 2 Yukon Gold)
- ½ teaspoon sea salt
- ¼ pound cheddar cheese, grated

Preparation:
1. Heat your cast-iron skillet over medium heat. Once it's hot, add the chorizo.

2. Cook for 8 to 10 minutes, frequently stirring, until browned and crisp.
3. Remove the chorizo from the skillet and set it aside.
4. Add the butter, onion, and garlic to the skillet.
5. Cook for 3 to 4 minutes until the onions have begun to soften.
6. Stir in the potatoes and salt and mix thoroughly.
7. Spread evenly, so the potatoes are distributed in a layer across the bottom of the pan.
8. Cook for 7 to 10 minutes until the potatoes have browned and crisped.
9. Use a spatula to flip the potatoes. Cook for an additional 5 to 7 minutes until the potatoes are browned on both sides.
10. Remove the skillet from the heat and stir in the cheese and chorizo.
11. Serve hot.
Serving Suggestion: Top with a runny fried egg or two.
Variation Tip: Substitute chorizo with spicy Italian sausage.
Nutritional Information per Serving:
Calories 422 | Fat 31.4g | Sodium 881mg | Carbs 15.2g | Fiber 2.4g | Sugar 2.2g | Protein 19.8g

Peanut Butter Oatmeal

Prep Time: 10 minutes
Cook Time: 45 minutes
Serves: 4
Ingredients:
• 2 cups rolled oats
• 2 ripe bananas, sliced
• 1 tablespoon packed brown sugar
• 1 teaspoon baking powder
• ½ teaspoon sea salt
• 2 eggs
• 1½ cups whole milk
• ¼ cup honey
• 3 tablespoons salted butter, room temperature
• ½ cup smooth peanut butter
Preparation:
1. Preheat the oven to 350°F.
2. Stir together the oats, bananas, brown sugar, baking powder, and salt in a large bowl.
3. Whisk together the eggs, milk, honey, and butter in a medium bowl.
4. Fold the milk mixture into the oat mixture. Spoon the batter into your cast-iron skillet.
5. Swirl half of the peanut butter into the batter, then top with the remaining half.

6. Bake for 40 to 45 minutes or until crisp around the edges and cooked through.
7. Serve hot.
Serving Suggestion: Top with berries and serve with cream.
Variation Tip: Substitute honey with maple syrup or agave.
Nutritional Information per Serving:
Calories 780 | Fat 40.9g | Sodium 471mg | Carbs 83.1g | Fiber 7.7g | Sugar 48g | Protein 27.8g

Onion and Sweet Potato Frittata

Prep Time: 10 minutes
Cook Time: 20 minutes
Serves: 6
Ingredients:
• 6 large eggs
• 1 cup shredded pepper jack cheese
• ¼ cup heavy whipping cream
• Pinch of sea salt
• 2 tablespoons salted butter
• 1 large sweet potato, peeled and cubed
• 1 white onion, chopped
• ½ teaspoon chipotle powder
• 2 garlic cloves, minced
Preparation:
1. Preheat the oven to 400°F.
2. Whisk the eggs, pepper jack cheese, cream, and salt to combine in a medium bowl. Set aside.
3. In a cast-iron skillet over medium heat, melt the butter.
4. Add the sweet potato, onion, and chipotle powder and stir to coat. Spread the sweet potato evenly across the skillet.
5. Cook for 3 to 4 minutes, then flip the sweet potato and cook for 2 to 3 minutes more. Stir in the garlic.
6. Pour the egg mixture over the sweet potato and stir to combine.
7. Cook for 1 to 2 minutes to set the eggs, then transfer the frittata to the oven.
8. Bake for 8 to 10 minutes, or until the eggs are set.
Serving Suggestion: Serve with Greek yogurt.
Variation Tip: The sweet potato can be grated if you prefer a smoother texture.
Nutritional Information per Serving:
Calories 218 | Fat 16.8g | Sodium 279mg | Carbs 9.2g | Fiber 1.4g | Sugar 3.4g | Protein 8.3g

Homemade Strawberry Clafoutis

Prep Time: 10 minutes
Cook Time: 25 minutes
Serves: 4
Ingredients:
• 2 cups fresh or frozen strawberries, halved or quartered
• 2 large eggs
• ½ gallon milk
• ½ cup unbleached all-purpose flour
• ¼ cup sugar
• ¼ teaspoon kosher salt
Preparation:
1. Preheat the oven to 375℉.
2. Arrange the berries in a single layer on the bottom of a cast-iron pan.
3. Whisk together the eggs, milk, flour, sugar, and salt in a mixing bowl.
4. Pour the mixture into the pan with the berries.
5. Bake for 25 minutes, or until the top is golden brown and the middle is set.
Serving Suggestion: Serve with soured cream and fresh strawberries.
Variation Tip: This may be made with almost any fruit: cherries, blueberries, nectarines, and peaches.
Nutritional Information per Serving:
Calories 373 | Fat 10.2g | Sodium 378mg | Carbs 54.9g | Fiber 1.9g | Sugar 39g | Protein 17.6g

Crispy Sweet Potatoes

Prep Time: 10 minutes
Cook Time: 15 minutes
Serves: 4
Ingredients:
• 1 large sweet potato, peeled and cubed into squares
• 2 tablespoons coconut oil
• 1 teaspoon chipotle powder
• 1 teaspoon sea salt.
Preparation:
1. In your cast iron skillet, melt the coconut oil over medium-high heat.
2. Add the sweet potato to the skillet in an even layer. Sprinkle with half the chipotle powder and half the salt.
3. Cook for 7 minutes until the sweet potato has browned and begins to soften.
4. Flip the potatoes, sprinkle on the remaining chipotle powder and salt, and cook for another 5 minutes, until the potatoes are soft, cooked through, and crisp around the edges.
5. Remove from the heat and serve warm.
Serving Suggestion: Top with a fried egg.
Variation Tip: These potatoes are delicious on their own but also wonderful in tacos, quesadillas, with eggs, or served as a side dish.
Nutritional Information per Serving:
Calories 227 | Fat 21.1g | Sodium 732mg | Carbs 10.1g | Fiber 1.5g | Sugar 3.7g | Protein 0.9g

Flavorful Shakshuka

Prep Time: 10 minutes
Cook Time: 45 minutes
Serves: 4
Ingredients:
• 1 tablespoon olive oil
• 1 white onion, chopped
• 3 garlic cloves, minced
• 1 jalapeño pepper, seeded and minced
• 2 tablespoons tomato paste
• 1 teaspoon smoked paprika
• ¼ teaspoon cayenne
• 1 teaspoon dried oregano
• 1 teaspoon ground cumin
• 1 teaspoon ground coriander
• ½ teaspoon sea salt
• ½ teaspoon freshly ground black pepper
• 1 (28-ounce) can diced tomatoes
• ½ cup vegetable broth, plus more if needed to thin sauce
• 4 eggs
• ¼ cup feta cheese, crumbled
• Handful fresh parsley, chopped
• Bread or pita, for serving
Preparation:
1. In your cast-iron pan, heat the oil over medium heat.

2. Add the onion, garlic, and jalapeño pepper to the pan.

3. Cook for 5 to 7 minutes, frequently stirring, until the onions brown.

4. Stir in the tomato paste, paprika, cayenne, oregano, cumin, coriander, salt, and pepper. Stir well all the ingredients into the tomato paste.

5. After 1 to 2 minutes of stirring constantly, add the diced tomatoes and vegetable broth. Stir well, then reduce the heat to a simmer.

6. Cook for 20 to 25 minutes. Taste your sauce and adjust the seasoning to your liking.

7. If it's too thick, add another ¼ cup of vegetable broth or water.

8. Crack the eggs into the sauce, cover the skillet, and increase the heat to medium.

9. Cook for 7 to 10 minutes for a soft yolk and 12 to 15 minutes for a firmer yolk.

10. Remove from the heat and top with the feta and parsley.

Serving Suggestion: Serve hot with warm bread or pita.

Variation Tip: Add more broth if you need to thin the sauce.

Nutritional Information per Serving:
Calories 187 | Fat 10.8g | Sodium 517mg | Carbs 14.7g | Fiber 4.1g | Sugar 8.4g | Protein 10.4g

Chees Tomato Frittata

Prep Time: 10 minutes
Cook Time: 25 minutes
Serves: 4
Ingredients:
• 8 eggs
• ⅔ cup Swiss cheese, shredded
• 1 cup cherry tomatoes, cut in half
• 3 cups fresh spinach
• 1 tablespoon butter
• ¼ teaspoon onion powder
• ¼ teaspoon garlic powder
• ¼ cup heavy cream
• Pepper
• Salt
Preparation:
1. Preheat the oven to 350°F.
2. In a mixing bowl, whisk the eggs with the onion powder, garlic powder, heavy cream, pepper, and salt.
3. Melt the butter in a pan over medium heat.
4. Once the butter is melted, add the spinach and stir until it wilts. Add to the egg mixture.
5. Add the cheese and tomatoes into the egg mixture and stir well to combine.

6. Spray a 9-inch cast-iron skillet with cooking spray. Pour the egg mixture into the skillet and bake it in the oven for 25–30 minutes.

Serving Suggestion: Slice and serve.

Variation Tip: You can substitute Swiss cheese with mozzarella, provolone, cheddar, or any other cheese you like.

Nutritional Information Per Serving:
Calories 260 | Fat 19.6g | Sodium 240mg | Carbs 4.7g | Fiber 1.1g | Sugar 2.3g | Protein 17.2g

Bacon and Asparagus Frittata

Prep Time: 10 minutes
Cook Time: 32 minutes
Serves: 8
Ingredients:
• 12 ounces bacon
• 2 cups fresh asparagus, sliced into 1-inch lengths
• 1 cup onion, finely chopped
• 2 garlic cloves, minced
• 10 eggs, beaten
• ¼ cup parsley, minced
• ½ teaspoon salt
• ¼ teaspoon ground black pepper
• 1 large tomato, sliced
• 1 cup cheddar cheese, shredded
Preparation:
1. In a 10-inch cast-iron skillet, brown the bacon until crispy, then transfer to a plate.
2. Cook the garlic, onion, and asparagus for 5 minutes in the same skillet.
3. Crumble the cooked bacon in a bowl and set aside a third of it.
4. Combine the eggs, bacon, black pepper, salt, and parsley in a mixing bowl.
5. Transfer this mixture to the same skillet.
6. Garnish with the reserved bacon, cheese, and tomato.
7. Cook for 15 minutes on medium-low heat, covered.
8. Cut into slices and serve.

Serving Suggestion: Serve with a side salad.

Variation Tip: Substitute bacon with ham.

Nutritional Information per Serving:
Calories 395 | Fat 28.8g | Sodium 1256mg | Carbs 5.2g | Fiber 1.4g | Sugar 2.4g | Protein 28.4sg

Creamy Mushrooms Au Gratin

Prep Time: 10 minutes
Cook Time: 16 minutes
Serves: 8
Ingredients:
• 2 tablespoons butter, melted
• 1-pound fresh mushrooms. sliced
• 1 green onion, chopped
For the sauce:
• 2 tablespoons melted butter
• 3 tablespoons all-purpose flour
• ¼ teaspoon salt
• ⅛ teaspoon ground black pepper
• 1-gallon milk
• ½ cup heavy whipping cream
• 2 tablespoon parmesan cheese, grated
For the eggs:
• 12 large eggs
• ¼ teaspoon salt
• ⅛ teaspoon black pepper, ground
• ¼ cup butter, cubed
• ½ cup parmesan cheese, grated
• 1 green onion, chopped
Preparation:
1. Sauté the mushrooms in the butter in a cast-iron pan for 6 minutes.
2. Add the green onion, cook for 1 minute, then transfer to a plate.
3. Combine the butter, salt, black pepper, and flour in the same pan to make the sauce.
4. Stir in the cream and milk and boil the mixture on low heat for 4 minutes, or until it thickens.
5. Add the cheese and let it melt before transferring the sauce to a bowl.
6. In a bowl, combine the eggs, black pepper, and salt.
7. Melt the butter in a second cast-iron pan and pour in the egg mixture.
8. Cook the eggs until they're set, and then top with the mushrooms, sauce, and cheese.
9. Bake the eggs in a preheated oven at 350℉ for 6 minutes.
10. Serve hot.
Serving Suggestion: Garnish with green onions.
Variation Tip: Substitute parmesan cheese with cheddar cheese.
Nutritional Information per Serving:
Calories 256 | Fat 17.9g | Sodium 397mg | Carbs 7g | Fiber 0.7g | Sugar 3.2g | Protein 18.1g

Cheese Orange Pancakes

Prep Time: 10 minutes
Cook Time: 20 minutes
Serves: 4
Ingredients:
• 4 large eggs, separated
• 1⅓ cups whole milk ricotta cheese
• 3 tablespoons granulated sugar
• 1½ tablespoons orange zest, freshly grated
• ½ cup all-purpose flour
• ½ teaspoon salt
• ¼ teaspoon cream of tartar
• 3 tablespoons unsalted butter, melted
Preparation:
1. Preheat the oven to 150ºF and line a baking sheet with foil.
2. Combine the egg yolks, ricotta, sugar, and orange zest in a mixing bowl and whisk until smooth.
3. Add the flour and whisk until combined; don't overmix.
4. Place the egg whites in a grease-free mixing bowl and beat at medium speed with an electric mixer until frothy.
5. Add the salt and cream of tartar, increase the speed to high, and beat until stiff peaks form.
6. Whisk ¼ of the meringue into the ricotta mixture and then fold in the remainder of the meringue.
7. Heat a 12-inch cast-iron skillet over medium-high heat.
8. Brush the skillet with some melted butter and add the pancake batter by ¼-cup measures, spreading the batter into 4-inch circles.
9. Cook the pancakes for 1½ to 2 minutes per side, or until golden.
10. Transfer the pancakes to the prepared baking sheet and keep them warm in the oven.
11. Cook the remaining pancakes in the same way, brushing the skillet with butter as necessary. Reduce the heat if the pancakes brown too quickly.
12. Serve hot.
Serving Suggestion: Serve with whipped cream and fresh berries.
Variation Tip: Feel free to add fresh berries of your choice to the pancake batter.
Nutritional Information per Serving:
Calories 561| Fat 31.8g | Sodium 707mg | Carbs 35.2g | Fiber 1.3g | Sugar 10.1g | Protein 34g

Onion Turkey Burgers

Prep Time: 10 minutes
Cook Time: 15 minutes
Serves: 4
Ingredients:
- 1-pound ground turkey
- ½ cup yellow onion, chopped
- ½ cup apple sauce
- 1 garlic clove
- 2 tablespoons butter
- 1 tablespoon olive oil
- ½ teaspoon salt
- ½ teaspoon pepper
- 4 whole-wheat English Muffins

Preparation:
1. Place the ground turkey and apple sauce in a bowl. Mix well. The apple sauce will keep the turkey burger moist. Add the salt and pepper.
2. Place a cast-iron skillet onto the stove, and pour in the oil. Set to a medium temperature, and heat the oil.
3. Mince the garlic, and place it in the cast-iron skillet. Wash, peel, and chop the onion.
4. Add the onion to the cast-iron skillet. Sauté the onions and garlic until tender, about 3 to 5 minutes.
5. Add the vegetables to the turkey, and mix thoroughly. Shape into balls and press a hole in the middle of each. Add ½ to 1 teaspoon of a dollop of butter in the centers.
6. Shape the turkey balls into patties, but make sure the butter is kept in the middle. Place back into the hot skillet, and turn the heat up to medium-high.
7. Cook the turkey burgers until they're cooked thoroughly, usually about 3 to 4 minutes on either side. While the turkey burgers are grilling, toast the English muffins.
8. Place the cooked turkey burger on top of the English muffin.
9. Serve warm.

Serving Suggestion: Garnish with your favorite toppings.
Variation Tip: Substitute ground turkey with ground chicken.
Nutritional Information per Serving:
Calories 450 | Fat 23.1g | Sodium 765mg | Carbs 29.9g | Fiber 4.9g | Sugar 7.3g | Protein 37.1g

Beef and Bean Casserole

Prep Time: 10 minutes
Cook Time: 30 minutes
Serves: 6
Ingredients:
- 1-pound ground beef
- 2 teaspoons canola oil
- Salt, to taste
- 2 tablespoons chili powder
- 4 garlic cloves, minced
- 2 cups (15-ounce can) black beans
- 1 teaspoon ground cumin
- 1¾ cups onion, chopped
- 2 cups (15-ounce can) diced tomatoes with jalapeño
- ½ cup cheddar cheese, shredded
- 1¾ cups white rice, cooked

Preparation:
1. In a 10-inch cast-iron skillet, add the oil. Place on the stove, set to medium-high heat, and heat the oil.
2. Add the onion to the skillet. Add the garlic and sauté until the onions are tender, about 3 to 5 minutes.
3. When the onions are tender, add the ground beef. Cook until the meat is brown, about 10 to 15 minutes.
4. Drain the beef, return it to the skillet, and then to the stove. Fold in the cumin. Add the salt and chili powder.
5. Drain the tomatoes, and add to the beef, mixing well.
6. Drain and rinse the black beans and stir until they're dispersed through the meat.
7. Fold in the rice, making sure the ingredients are well mixed.
8. Cook for an additional 2 to 5 minutes or until the dish is heated.
9. Shred the cheese, and add to the top of the meat. Cover with a lid, and allow to cook for another 2 minutes.
10. Remove from heat and serve warm.

Serving Suggestion: Serve with the cooked white rice.
Variation Tip: Omit chili powder for a milder taste.
Nutritional Information per Serving:
Calories 642 | Fat 11.2g | Sodium 296ag | Carbs 90.2g | Fiber 12.5g | Sugar 3.8g | Protein 44.3g

Garlic Chicken Thighs

Prep Time: 10 minutes
Cook Time: 30 minutes
Serves: 4
Ingredients:
- 8 chicken thighs
- 2 tablespoons canola oil
- ¼ teaspoon paprika
- 1 teaspoon garlic powder
- Pepper
- Salt

Preparation:
1. Preheat the oven to 425°F.
2. Season the chicken thighs with paprika, garlic powder, salt, and pepper.
3. Heat the oil in a cast-iron skillet over medium-high heat.
4. Place the chicken into the skillet and cook for 8–9 minutes.
5. Flip the chicken and roast it in the preheated oven for 20 minutes or until the internal temperature of the chicken reaches 165°F.

Serving Suggestion: Garnish the chicken with freshly chopped parsley and serve.
Variation Tip: You can add your choice of seasonings.
Nutritional Information Per Serving:
Calories 619 | Fat 28.7g | Sodium 290mg | Carbs 0.6g | Fiber 0.1g | Sugar 0.2g | Protein 84.6g

Juicy Butter Chicken Breast

Prep Time: 10 minutes
Cook Time: 15 minutes
Serves: 4
Ingredients:
- 4 boneless chicken breasts
- ¼ cup butter
- ½ teaspoon onion powder
- ½ teaspoon oregano

- 1 teaspoon garlic powder
- 1 teaspoon paprika
- 2 tablespoons canola oil
- Salt

Preparation:
1. Mix the paprika, garlic powder, oregano, onion powder, and salt in a small bowl.
2. Rub the chicken with the spice mixture.
3. Heat the oil in a cast-iron skillet over medium heat.
4. Place the chicken into the skillet and cook until lightly browned. Add the butter and cook the chicken until its internal temperature reaches 165°F.

Serving Suggestion: Slice the chicken and serve with a side salad.
Variation Tip: You can also add your choice of seasonings.
Nutritional Information Per Serving:
Calories 357 | Fat 23.5g | Sodium 197mg | Carbs 0.9g | Fiber 0.3g | Sugar 0.3g | Protein 34.1g

Wok-Fried Turkey Strips with Mushrooms

Prep Time: 15 minutes
Cook Time: 20 minutes
Serves: 2
Ingredients:
- 1 garlic clove, minced
- 1 tablespoon butter
- ½ pound turkey breast, boneless, skinless, cut into 2-inch strips
- ¾ cup beef broth
- ⅛ teaspoon salt
- 2 cups fresh mushrooms, sliced
- 1 tablespoon tomato paste

Preparation:
1. In a large-sized cast-iron wok, melt the butter over medium heat and sauté the garlic for about 1 minute.
2. Add the turkey and cook for about 5–6 minutes or until cooked through.
3. Put the turkey strips onto a plate.
4. In the same wok, add the mushrooms and cook for about 6 minutes.
5. Add the broth, tomato paste, and salt and cook for about 5 minutes, stirring occasionally.
6. Stir in the cooked turkey strips and cook for about 3 minutes.
7. Serve hot.

Serving Suggestion: Serve alongside garlic aioli.
Variation Tip: You can use chicken instead.
Nutritional Information per Serving:
Calories: 199|Fat: 7g|Sat Fat: 1.7g|Carbohydrates: 4.7g|Fiber: 1.1g|Sugar: 2.5g|Protein: 32.6g

Rosemary Chicken Breasts

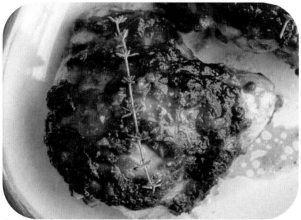

Prep Time: 10 minutes
Cook Time: 25 minutes
Serves: 4
Ingredients:
• 1-pound chicken breasts, cut in half
• ½ cup fig preserves
• ½ cup balsamic glaze
• 2 rosemary sprigs
• 1 tablespoon garlic, minced
• ¼ cup butter
• Pepper
• Salt
Preparation:
1. Preheat the oven to 425°F.
2. Mix the butter, half the rosemary, half the garlic, pepper, and salt in a small bowl, then rub the mixture over the chicken.
3. Add the chicken to a 9-inch cast-iron skillet and cook in the preheated oven for 10 minutes.
4. Mix the fig preserves, glaze, remaining garlic, and rosemary in a separate bowl.
5. Brush the chicken with the fig preserve mixture and cook for 10–15 minutes more or until the internal temperature of the chicken reaches 165°F.
Serving Suggestion: Pour the remaining fig mixture over the chicken and serve.
Variation Tip: You can also use chicken thighs instead of chicken breasts.
Nutritional Information Per Serving:
Calories 383 | Fat 22.8g | Sodium 336mg | Carbs 5.6g | Fiber 1.3g | Sugar 2.8g | Protein 38g

Lemon Chicken Fajitas

Prep Time: 10 minutes
Cook Time: 15 minutes
Serves: 4
Ingredients:
• 1-pound boneless chicken breasts, cut into slices
• 5 tablespoons canola oil
• 2 bell peppers, sliced
• 1 onion, sliced
• 2 teaspoons garlic powder
• 2 teaspoons cumin powder
• 1 tablespoon chili powder
• 2 tablespoons lemon juice
• Pepper
• Salt
Preparation:
1. Add the chicken, garlic powder, cumin powder, chili powder, lemon juice, 4 tablespoons of oil, salt, and pepper salt into a sealable bag. Shake the sealed bag well and place it into the refrigerator to marinate overnight.
2. Remove the chicken from the marinade and add it to a cast-iron skillet. Set the marinade aside. Cook the chicken over medium-high heat for 6–8 minutes. Transfer the chicken to a plate and set it aside.
3. Heat the remaining oil in the same skillet over medium heat.
4. Add the bell peppers, onion, and reserved marinade and cook for 5–7 minutes.
5. Return the chicken to the skillet and cook for 2–4 minutes.
Serving Suggestion: Garnish with parsley and serve.
Variation Tip: You can also add your choice of seasonings.
Nutritional Information Per Serving:
Calories 417 | Fat 26.7g | Sodium 162mg | Carbs 9.8g | Fiber 2.3g | Sugar 4.8g | Protein 34.4g

Rosemary Chicken Thighs

Prep Time: 10 minutes
Cook Time: 45 minutes
Serves: 6
Ingredients:
• 6 chicken thighs
• 1 lemon, cut into wedges
• 1 bay leaf
• 1 tablespoon garlic, chopped
• 3 fresh rosemary sprigs
• ½ cup chicken stock
• 1½ cups white wine

- ¼ cup canola oil
- 1 cup flour
- Pepper
- Salt

Preparation:
1. Preheat the oven to 425°F.
2. Season the chicken with salt and pepper and coat it with the flour.
3. Heat the oil in a 12-inch cast-iron skillet over medium-high heat.
4. Add the chicken to the skillet and cook for 5 minutes or until browned.
5. Turn the chicken. Add the bay leaf, garlic, rosemary, stock, and wine and cook for 2 minutes.
6. Add the lemon around the chicken and bake in the preheated oven for 30 minutes.

Serving Suggestion: Garnish with fresh parsley and serve.

Variation Tip: You can also use chicken broth instead of stock.

Nutritional Information Per Serving:
Calories 491 | Fat 20.3g | Sodium 220mg | Carbs 19.4g | Fiber 1.2g | Sugar 0.8g | Protein 44.7g

Baked Chicken and Potato with Parsley

Prep Time: 10 minutes
Cook Time: 30 minutes
Serves: 4
Ingredients:
- 6 chicken thighs
- ¾ cup parmesan cheese, shredded
- ½ cup chicken stock
- ½ tablespoon parsley, minced
- 1 tablespoon fresh rosemary, minced
- ½ teaspoon paprika
- 1 tablespoon garlic, minced
- 2 tablespoons butter
- 1 teaspoon canola oil
- 2 potatoes, cut into small pieces
- Pepper
- Salt

Preparation:
1. Preheat the oven to 400°F.
2. Mix the butter, herbs, paprika, garlic, pepper, and salt in a bowl and set aside.
3. Heat the oil in a cast-iron skillet over medium heat.
4. Add the chicken to the skillet and sear for 3–5 minutes over medium-high heat. Season the chicken with salt and pepper.

5. Turn the chicken and add the potatoes, stock, and butter mixture. Combine everything well.
6. Sprinkle the parmesan cheese over the top of the chicken and bake in the preheated oven for 20–25 minutes.

Serving Suggestion: Garnish with fresh parsley and serve.

Variation Tip: You can also add white wine instead of chicken stock.

Nutritional Information Per Serving:
Calories 613 | Fat 27.1g | Sodium 527mg | Carbs 18.8g | Fiber 3.1g | Sugar 1.4g | Protein 70.9g

Thyme Duck Breast Slices

Prep Time: 10 minutes
Cook Time: 16 minutes
Serves: 2
Ingredients:
- 2 shallots, sliced thinly
- 1 tablespoon fresh ginger, minced
- 2 tablespoons fresh thyme, chopped
- Salt and ground black pepper, as required
- 2 duck breasts

Preparation:
1. Place the ginger, shallots, thyme, salt, and black pepper in a large bowl, and mix well.
2. Add the duck breasts and coat them evenly with the marinade.
3. Refrigerate the marinated duck breasts for about 12 hours.
4. Preheat a greased cast-iron grill pan over medium-high heat.
5. Place the duck breasts onto the grill pan, skin-side down, and cook for about 8 minutes per side.
6. Serve hot.

Serving Suggestion: Serve alongside fresh greens.

Variation Tip: You can also add fresh rosemary to this recipe.

Nutritional Information per Serving:
Calories: 337|Fat: 10.1g|Sat Fat: 2.5g|Carbohydrates: 3.4g|Fiber: 0g|Sugar: 0.1g|Protein: 55.5g

Parmesan Chicken Casserole

Prep Time: 10 minutes
Cook Time: 20 minutes
Serves: 4
Ingredients:
• 1-pound chicken breasts, cut into cubes
• 1 teaspoon dried basil
• 1 cup mozzarella cheese, shredded
• 1 cup parmesan cheese, grated
• 1 cup breadcrumbs
• 1 cup marinara sauce
• 2 tablespoons canola oil
• 1 tablespoon Italian seasoning
• Pepper
• Salt
Preparation:
1. Preheat the oven to 350°F.
2. Heat the oil in a cast-iron skillet over medium heat.
3. Add the chicken to the skillet and season with the onion powder, Italian seasoning, pepper, and salt, and stir well. Cook the chicken over medium heat for 5 minutes.
4. Add the marinara sauce and stir well.
5. Add the basil, breadcrumbs, mozzarella, and parmesan over the chicken and cook it in the preheated oven for 15 minutes.
Serving Suggestion: Garnish with parsley and serve.
Variation Tip: Add ½ teaspoon of red chili flakes.
Nutritional Information Per Serving:
Calories 492 | Fat 22.3g | Sodium 699mg | Carbs 28.9g | Fiber 2.9g | Sugar 7.5g | Protein 41.8g

Creamy Chicken Thighs

Prep Time: 10 minutes
Cook Time: 30 minutes
Serves: 4
Ingredients:
• 2 pounds' chicken thighs
• ⅓ cup chicken stock
• ⅓ cup heavy cream
• 1 large onion, sliced
• 2 tablespoons butter
• 1 teaspoon canola oil
• 1 teaspoon garlic powder
• ½ teaspoon ground thyme
• 1 teaspoon Creole seasoning
• Pepper
• Salt
Preparation:
1. Preheat the oven to 350°F.
2. Season the chicken with the garlic powder, thyme, Creole seasoning, salt, and pepper.
3. Heat the oil in a cast-iron skillet over medium-high heat.
4. Add the chicken to the skillet and sear for 2 minutes on each side. Transfer the chicken to a plate and set it aside.
5. Melt the butter in the same skillet over medium heat.
6. Add the onions to the skillet and sauté until the onion is softened.
7. Turn the heat to medium-low. Add the cream and stock and stir for 2–3 minutes.
8. Return the chicken to the skillet and bake in the preheated oven for 20–25 minutes.
Serving Suggestion: Garnish with parsley and serve.
Variation Tip: You can also add chicken broth instead of stock.
Nutritional Information Per Serving:
Calories 545 | Fat 27.6g | Sodium 614mg | Carbs 4.5g | Fiber 0.9g | Sugar 1.8g | Protein 66.5g

Roasted Chicken with Leeks

Prep Time: 15 minutes
Cook Time: 1 hour
Serves: 6
Ingredients:
• 1 (4-pound) whole chicken, neck and giblets removed
• 3 leeks (white and pale green parts), halved lengthwise
• Salt and black pepper, to taste
• 3 tablespoons olive oil, divided
Preparation:

1. Season the chicken with salt, inside and out, generously.
2. Tie the legs together with kitchen twine. Leave out at room temperature for about 1 hour.
3. Preheat the oven to 425°F. Arrange a rack in the upper third of the oven.
4. Put a 12-inch cast-iron wok in a baking dish and place them into the oven to preheat.
5. Meanwhile, add the leeks, 2 tablespoons of oil, salt, and black pepper to a bowl and toss to coat well.
6. Using paper towels, pat the chicken dry and coat it with half of the remaining oil.
7. Place the remaining oil in the hot wok and spread it out evenly.
8. Arrange the chicken in the center of the wok and place the leeks around it.
9. Roast for about 60 minutes.
10. Remove from the oven and set aside for about 5 minutes before carving.
11. With a sharp knife, cut the chicken into de-sired-sized pieces and serve.
Serving Suggestion: Serve with mashed potatoes.
Variation Tip: You can also use turkey meat for this recipe.
Nutritional Information per Serving:
Calories: 654|Fat: 44.9g|Sat Fat: 7.5g|Carbohydrates: 6.3g|Fiber: 0.8g|Sugar: 1.7g|Protein: 54.7g

Chicken Breasts with Spinach Stuffing

Prep Time: 10 minutes
Cook Time: 25 minutes
Serves: 4
Ingredients:
• 1½ cups fresh spinach, chopped
• ⅓ cup sun-dried tomatoes, chopped
• ¼ cup goat's cheese, crumbled
• 2 garlic cloves, minced
• ½ teaspoon ground black pepper
• ¼ teaspoon salt
• 2 boneless, skinless chicken breasts (6 ounces)
Preparation:
1. Preheat the oven to 400°F.
2. Combine the spinach, ⅛ teaspoon of salt, ¼ teaspoon of black pepper, garlic, goat's cheese, and sun-dried tomatoes in a mixing bowl.
3. Cut the chicken breasts horizontally on one side to create a pocket.
4. Stuff each chicken pocket with an equal amount of the spinach mixture and secure it with a toothpick.

5. Preheat a cast-iron skillet with 1 tablespoon of oil over medium heat.
6. Sear the chicken on both sides for a few minutes or until golden brown.
7. Place in the oven and bake for 25 minutes or until cooked through.
8. Serve immediately.
Serving Suggestion: Serve with a side of vegetables.
Variation Tip: Switch up fresh spinach with frozen chopped spinach.
Nutritional Information per Serving:
Calories 207 | Fat 10.9g | Sodium 344 mg | Carbs 4.5g | Fiber 1.5g | Sugar 1.8g | Protein 23.1g

Roasted Whole Chicken

Prep Time: 1 hour 10 minutes
Cook Time: 1 hour
Serves: 6
Ingredients:
• 1 whole chicken
• 4 tablespoons salted butter, room temperature
• 10 garlic cloves
• 1 tablespoon sea salt
• 2 tablespoons olive oil, divided
• 1 tablespoon dried oregano
• 1 tablespoon fresh rosemary, minced
Preparation:
1. Tie the chicken legs together for even roasting.
2. Preheat the oven to 475°F.
3. Rub the chicken with the butter, working it all over the skin and into the folds.
4. Cut ten slits, about 1-inch deep, through the chicken breasts and legs. Stuff a garlic clove into each slit.
5. Sprinkle with salt.
6. Coat your cast-iron skillet with one tablespoon of olive oil and place the chicken in it.
7. Drizzle with the remaining olive oil and top with oregano and rosemary.
8. Place the skillet in the oven, cook for 20 minutes, and then drop the temperature to 400°F.
9. Cook for an additional 40 minutes.
10. Remove the skillet from the oven and let the chicken rest for 10 minutes before serving.
Serving Suggestion: Serve with green beans.
Variation Tip: Feel free to add more herbs like thyme, tarragon, and parsley.
Nutritional Information per Serving:
Calories 953 | Fat 70.9g | Sodium 992mg | Carbs 2.5g | Fiber 0.7g | Sugar 0.1g | Protein 83.8g

Orange Chicken Breast Slices

Prep Time: 10 minutes
Cook Time: 20 minutes
Serves: 4
Ingredients:
• 1-pound boneless, skinless chicken breast, sliced into 1½-inch slices (3 breasts)
• 2 oranges
• 2 tablespoons soy sauce, divided
• 2 garlic cloves, minced
• ½ cup cornstarch plus 2 teaspoons
• 2 teaspoons dry sherry
• ¼ teaspoon crushed red pepper
• 2 cups canola oil plus 1 tablespoon
• 2 tablespoons sugar
• 1 teaspoon rice vinegar
• 2 teaspoons fresh ginger, minced
Preparation:
1. In a bowl, add the chicken, one tablespoon of soy sauce, and one teaspoon of sherry, then toss until the chicken is coated.
2. Place in the fridge, and allow it to sit for about 30 minutes.
3. Place a 10-inch cast-iron skillet onto the stove, and set the temperature to medium.
4. Pour in enough of the 2 cups of oil to fill the pan about a 1/2 -inch deep. You may not need the full 2 cups.
5. Add ½ cup of cornstarch to a small bowl.
6. Remove the chicken from the sauce, and dip it in the cornstarch. Turn the chicken until it's completely coated. Knock off any excess cornstarch.
7. Place the chicken into the hot oil, making sure not to overcrowd. You may have to do several batches.
8. Cook the chicken, turning several times until it's a deep golden brown and is cooked completely through, about 5 to 10 minutes.
9. Remove the chicken from the oil and drain it on a paper towel.
10. Use a vegetable peeler, and make four strips of orange zest. You want them to be about 3 to 4 inches in length. Place the zest between two layers of paper towels.
11. Microwave the zests for about 80 seconds.
12. Remove from the microwave and cool completely. Once the zest is cooled, dice it, and set it aside.
13. Squeeze the juice from both oranges. Use additional oranges if necessary. You'll need about a ½ cup of juice.

14. Pour the juice into a bowl, and add two teaspoons of cornstarch. Stir until the cornstarch is completely dissolved. Set aside.
15. In a separate 10-inch cast-iron skillet, heat one tablespoon of oil. Set the temperature to medium heat.
16. Add the garlic and ginger to the skillet.
17. Stir in the dried orange zest and the crushed red pepper.
18. Sauté for about 30 seconds or until they're golden brown. Whisk together the soy sauce and sugar. Add the vinegar and sherry and mix thoroughly.
19. Pour into the garlic mixture, and stir until the sugar has completely dissolved. Add the orange juice mixture.
20. Bring the garlic mixture to a boil, and then reduce heat to low. Simmer for a minute, stirring continuously.
21. Slowly add the fried chicken, adding water if it's too thick. Stir constantly until the dish is hot and the chicken is coated. This usually takes about 3 to 5 minutes.
22. Serve warm.
Serving Suggestion: Serve with rice.
Variation Tip: Substitute rice vinegar with apple cider vinegar.
Nutritional Information per Serving:
Calories 752 | Fat 57.5g | Sodium 511mg | Carbs 33.3g | Fiber 2.6g | Sugar 14.8g | Protein 25.6g

Orange-Flavored Duck with Bok Choy

Prep Time: 15 minutes
Cook Time: 12 minutes
Serves: 6
Ingredients:
• 2 tablespoons coconut oil
• ⅔ cup orange juice, freshly squeezed
• ¼ cup chicken broth
• 1 onion, thinly sliced
• 2 teaspoons fresh ginger, finely grated
• 1 tablespoon fresh orange zest, finely grated
• 2 pounds bok choy leaves
• 2 garlic cloves, minced

- 1½ pounds cooked duck meat, chopped
- 1 orange, peeled, seeded, and segmented

Preparation:
1. In a large cast-iron wok, melt the coconut oil over medium heat and sauté the onion, ginger, and garlic for about 3 minutes.
2. Add the ginger and garlic and sauté for about 2 minutes
3. Stir in the orange zest, broth, and orange juice and bring to a boil.
4. Add the duck meat and cook for about 3 minutes.
5. Transfer the duck meat to a plate.
6. In the same wok, add the bok choy and cook for about 4 minutes.
7. Divide the bok choy mixture onto serving plates and top with the duck meat.

Serving Suggestion: Serve with the garnishing of orange segments over a bed of noodles.
Variation Tip: You can also use beef broth instead of chicken broth.
Nutritional Information per Serving:
Calories: 337|Fat: 17.9g|Sat Fat: 2.3g|Carbohydrates: 14.2g|Fiber: 3.7g|Sugar: 8.7g|Protein: 31g

Scrambled Chicken with Bell Peppers and Pineapple

Prep Time: 15 minutes
Cook Time: 20 minutes
Serves: 4
Ingredients:
- 1 large onion, chopped
- 1 teaspoon fresh ginger, minced
- 1 tablespoon extra-virgin olive oil
- 1 garlic clove, minced
- 2 chicken breasts, skinless, boneless, and cubed
- 2 tomatoes, seeded and chopped
- 1 green bell pepper, seeded and chopped
- 2 tablespoons soy sauce
- Ground black pepper, to taste
- 2 cups fresh pineapple, cubed
- 1 medium red bell pepper, seeded and chopped
- 1 medium orange bell pepper, seeded and chopped
- 1 tablespoon apple cider vinegar

Preparation:
1. Heat the oil over medium heat in a large cast-iron wok and sauté the onion for about 5 minutes.
2. Add the garlic and ginger and sauté for about 1 minute.
3. Add the chicken and cook for about 5 minutes or until browned on all sides.

4. Add the tomatoes, pineapple, and bell peppers and cook for about 6 minutes until the vegetables become tender.
5. Add the vinegar, soy sauce, and black pepper and cook for about 3 minutes.
6. Serve hot.

Serving Suggestion: Serve with crusty bread.
Variation Tip: Use leafy greens of your choice.
Nutritional Information per Serving:
Calories: 296|Fat: 10.3g|Sat Fat: 2.7g|Carbohydrates: 26.4g|Fiber: 4.1g|Sugar: 16g|Protein: 27.9g

Flavorful Chicken Cutlets with Cracker Mixture

Prep Time: 10 minutes
Cook Time: 20 minutes
Serves: 4
Ingredients:
- 2 eggs
- 4 chicken cutlets, sliced
- 1 tablespoon butter
- 2 tablespoons canola oil
- 1 teaspoon Italian seasoning
- ¼ teaspoon paprika
- ½ teaspoon garlic powder
- 1 cup crackers, crushed
- Pepper
- Salt

Preparation:
1. Preheat the oven to 400°F.
2. Mix the crushed crackers, garlic powder, paprika, Italian seasoning, pepper, and salt in a shallow dish.
3. Add the eggs to a small bowl and whisk well.
4. Heat the oil and butter in a cast-iron skillet over medium heat.
5. Dip each chicken slice in the egg and coat with the cracker mixture.
6. Place the coated chicken into the skillet and cook until browned on all sides, then place the skillet in the preheated oven and bake until the internal temperature of the chicken reaches 165°F.

Serving Suggestion: Serve the chicken cutlets with your choice of dip.
Variation Tip: You can also use vegetable oil instead of canola oil.
Nutritional Information Per Serving:
Calories 479 | Fat 27.2g | Sodium 347mg | Carbs 10.1g | Fiber 0.3g | Sugar 0.7g | Protein 46.3g

Delicious Sweet and Sour Chicken

Prep Time: 10 minutes
Cook Time: 25 minutes
Serves: 4
Ingredients:
- ⅓ cup apple cider vinegar
- ¼ cup ketchup
- 2 tablespoons soy sauce
- 1 tablespoon sriracha
- 1 tablespoon light brown sugar
- 1 (8-ounce) can pineapple chunks, strained, ¾ cup juice reserved, divided
- 2 boneless, skinless chicken breasts, cut into chunks
- ¼ cup cornstarch
- 1 teaspoon sea salt, divided
- ⅓ cup vegetable oil, divided
- 1 large white onion, minced
- 1 red bell pepper, cut into strips
- 1 green bell pepper, cut into strips
- 4 garlic cloves, minced
- 1 tablespoon peeled, minced fresh ginger
- Steamed rice, for serving

Preparation:
1. In a small bowl, whisk the vinegar, ketchup, soy sauce, sriracha, brown sugar, and ¼ cup of reserved pineapple juice until smooth. Set aside.
2. Combine the chicken, cornstarch, and ½ teaspoon of salt in a medium bowl. Coat the chicken thoroughly with the cornstarch.
3. Heat 2 tablespoons of oil in the cast-iron skillet over medium-high heat.
4. Add the chicken and spread it evenly across the bottom of the skillet. Cook for 3 to 4 minutes, or until browned.
5. Flip and cook for 2 to 3 minutes more. Remove the chicken from the skillet and set it on a rack to drain any excess oil.
6. Pour in the remaining oil and add the onion. Stir, making sure nothing sticks to the skillet, and cook for 3 to 4 minutes or until the onion is tender.
7. Add the red and green bell peppers and cook for 1 to 2 minutes, or until slightly charred.
8. Add the pineapple chunks and cook for 1 to 2 minutes, until browned.
9. Stir in the garlic and ginger and cook for 1 minute, stirring well.
10. Return the chicken to the skillet and stir, then add the sauce.
11. Stir well, so the sauce completely coats the chicken and vegetables. Cook for 2 to 3 minutes, occasionally stirring, until the sauce thickens.
12. Serve hot.

Serving Suggestion: Serve over rice.
Variation Tip: Substitute apple cider vinegar with balsamic vinegar.
Nutritional Information per Serving:
Calories 354 | Fat 19.3g | Sodium 1157mg | Carbs 31.4g | Fiber 2.9g | Sugar 15.3g | Protein 15.4g

Wok-Fried Chicken Breasts with Cabbage

Prep Time: 15 minutes
Cook Time: 20 minutes
Serves: 4
Ingredients:
- 3 garlic cloves, minced
- 1-pound chicken breasts, boneless, skinless, cut into bite-sized pieces
- 5 cups green cabbage, shredded
- 2 tablespoons olive oil, divided
- ½ large onion, chopped
- ½ large green bell pepper, seeded and chopped
- ½ teaspoon ground ginger
- Ground black pepper, to taste
- ¼ cup low-sodium soy sauce
- 2 tablespoons fresh chives, chopped

Preparation:
1. Heat 1 tablespoon of oil over medium heat in a large cast-iron wok and sauté the garlic for about 30 seconds.
2. Add the onion and cook for about 7 minutes, stirring frequently.
3. Now, add the remaining oil over medium-high heat and stir fry the chicken pieces for about 5 minutes.
4. Stir in the cabbage, bell pepper, ground ginger, soy sauce, and black pepper, and stir fry for about 5 minutes.
Serving Suggestions: Serve hot with the garnishing of chives.
Variation Tip: You can also use tamari instead of soy sauce.
Nutritional Information per Serving:
Calories: 329|Fat: 15.6g|Sat Fat: 3.4g|Carbohydrates: 12g|Fiber: 2.9g|Sugar: 4.4g|Protein: 34.4g

Lemony Butter Chicken

Prep Time: 10 minutes
Cook Time: 15 minutes
Serves: 4
Ingredients:
- 2 chicken breasts, cut in half
- 2 tablespoons fresh lemon juice
- ½ tablespoon lemon zest
- 1 tablespoon canola oil
- ½ cup chicken stock
- 3 tablespoons butter
- ¼ teaspoon garlic powder
- ¼ cup flour
- Pepper
- Salt

Preparation:
1. Season the chicken with the garlic powder, pepper, and salt, and coat with the flour.
2. Heat the oil and 1 tablespoon of butter in a cast-iron skillet over medium-high heat.
3. Add the chicken to the skillet and cook for 4–5 minutes on each side. Transfer the chicken to a plate and set it aside.
4. Add the stock, lemon zest, remaining butter, and lemon juice in the same skillet and cook for a couple of minutes.
5. Return the chicken to the skillet and cook until the chicken is completely done.

Serving Suggestion: Garnish with parsley and serve.
Variation Tip: You can also add chicken broth instead of stock.
Nutritional Information Per Serving:
Calories 278 | Fat 17.8g | Sodium 260mg | Carbs 6.5g | Fiber 0.3g | Sugar 0.3g | Protein 22.2g

Garlicky Turkey Stir-Fry

Prep Time: 10 minutes
Cook Time: 12 minutes
Serves: 2
Ingredients:
- ½ pound turkey meat, diced
- 1 tablespoon oyster sauce, divided
- ½-inch piece fresh ginger root, finely chopped, divided
- 1 tablespoon Chinese cooking wine, divided
- ½ tablespoon vegetable oil
- ½ tablespoon garlic, minced
- 6-ounce canned lychees, drained
- 1 red chili pepper, seeded and sliced into strips
- ½ tablespoon soy sauce
- 1 dash ground black pepper, for garnish
- ½ bunch fresh cilantro, chopped, for garnish
- ½ bunch green onions, chopped, for garnish

Preparation:
1. In a bowl, combine half of the Chinese cooking wine, half of the oyster sauce, and half of the ginger.
2. Marinate the turkey in the mixture for 30 minutes.
3. Heat the oil in a cast-iron skillet and add the garlic.
4. Cook until browned.
5. Add the turkey with the marinade and the rest of the ingredients, except the garnishes.
6. Cook for 5 to 10 minutes or until cooked through.
7. Serve.

Serving Suggestion: Serve over rice and add the garnishes.
Variation Tip: Switch up the oyster sauce with hoisin sauce.
Nutritional Information per Serving:
Calories 298 | Fat 9.6g | Sodium 367mg | Carbs 17.6g | Fiber 1.6g | Sugar 14.3g | Protein 34.8g

Garlic Chicken Thighs with Mushroom

Prep Time: 10 minutes
Cook Time: 20 minutes
Serves: 6
Ingredients:
- 1½ pounds boneless and skinless chicken thighs
- 1 tablespoon garlic, minced
- 3 tablespoons butter
- 8 ounces' white mushrooms, sliced
- 2 tablespoons canola oil
- ½ teaspoon red pepper flakes, crushed

- 1 teaspoon paprika
- 1 teaspoon garlic powder
- 1 teaspoon onion powder
- Pepper
- Salt

Preparation:
1. Mix the red pepper flakes, paprika, garlic powder, pepper, onion powder, and salt in a small bowl.
2. Rub the spice mixture over the chicken.
3. Heat the canola oil in a cast-iron skillet over medium heat.
4. Place the chicken into the skillet and cook for 8 minutes. Turn the chicken and cook it for 8 minutes more or until its internal temperature reaches 165°F.
5. Transfer the chicken to a plate.
6. Melt the butter in the same skillet. Add the mushrooms and sauté for 3–4 minutes, then season with salt and pepper.
7. Add the garlic and sauté for a minute. Return the chicken to the skillet and mix well.

Serving Suggestion: Garnish with parsley and serve.
Variation Tip: You can also use cremini mushrooms instead of white mushrooms.
Nutritional Information Per Serving:
Calories 322 | Fat 19g | Sodium 168mg | Carbs 2.7g | Fiber 0.7g | Sugar 1g | Protein 34.3g

Baked Chicken Thighs

Prep Time: 10 minutes
Cook Time: 22 minutes
Serves: 6
Ingredients:
- 6 (6-ounce) skin-on, bone-in chicken thighs
- 1 tablespoon vegetable oil
- Salt and black pepper, as required

Preparation:
1. Preheat the oven to 475°F.
2. Season the chicken thighs evenly with salt and black pepper.
3. In a 12-inch cast-iron wok, heat the oil over high heat.
4. Put the chicken thighs in the wok, skin side down, and cook for about 2 minutes, flipping occasionally.

5. Transfer the wok to the oven and bake for about 13 minutes.
6. Flip the chicken thighs and bake for another 5 minutes.
7. Serve hot.

Serving Suggestion: Serve the chicken thighs with your choice of dip.
Variation Tip: You can also try this recipe with chicken breasts.
Nutritional Information per Serving:
Calories: 294|Fat: 12.7g|Sat Fat: 1.8g|Carbohydrates: 0g|Fiber: 0g|Sugar: 0g|Protein: 42.4g

Lemony Turkey Breast

Prep Time: 10 minutes
Cook Time: 1 hour 30 minutes
Serves: 4
Ingredients:
- 1 whole bone-in turkey breast
- 8 tablespoons (1 stick) butter, at room temperature
- 4 garlic cloves, minced
- 2 teaspoons sea salt
- 1 teaspoon chipotle powder
- 2 large onions, cut into rings
- ½ cup white wine
- ½ cup chicken broth
- Juice of 2 lemons

Preparation:
1. Clean the turkey breast and pat it dry.
2. Preheat the oven to 325°F.
3. Stir together the butter, garlic, salt, and chipotle powder in a small bowl.
4. Spread the butter mixture over the turkey, really working it into and under the skin wherever possible.
5. Arrange the onions on the bottom of a cast-iron skillet.
6. Pour in the white wine and broth.
7. Place the turkey on top of the onions.
8. Roast for 1 hour and 30 minutes, until the skin browns and crisps, the turkey's internal temperature reaches 165°F, and the juices run clear.
9. Let it rest for 10 minutes before carving and serving.

Serving Suggestion: Garnish with rosemary sprigs.
Variation Tip: Substitute butter with olive or avocado oil.
Nutritional Information per Serving:
Calories 439 | Fat 31.7g | Sodium 1336mg | Carbs 11g | Fiber 1.8g | Sugar 6.4g | Protein 20g

Chicken Marsala with Parsley

Prep Time: 10 minutes
Cook Time: 35 minutes
Serves: 4
Ingredients:
• 1½ cups chicken broth
• 1½ cups Marsala wine
• 4 boneless, skinless chicken breasts
• 2 tablespoons olive oil, plus more as needed
• ½ cup all-purpose flour
• 1½ teaspoons sea salt, divided
• 3 tablespoons salted butter
• 2 cups sliced cremini mushrooms
• 3 garlic cloves, minced
• ¼ teaspoon freshly ground black pepper
• 1 teaspoon fresh thyme leaves, minced
• 1 teaspoon fresh oregano leaves, minced
• ¼ cup heavy (whipping) cream
• Minced fresh parsley leaves, for garnish
• Lemon wedges, for garnish
Preparation:
1. Combine the broth and wine in a medium saucepan over high heat. Bring to a light boil, then reduce the heat to low and let simmer for 7 minutes.
2. On a cutting board and using a meat tenderizer, flatten the chicken to an even thickness.
3. Heat the oil in a cast-iron skillet over medium-high heat.
4. Stir together the flour and ½ teaspoon of salt in a shallow bowl. Dredge both sides of the chicken in the flour.
5. Place the chicken into the skillet and cook for 5 to 6 minutes, flip, and cook for 5 to 6 minutes more, adding more oil as needed. Set the chicken aside to cool.
6. In the skillet over medium heat, melt the butter. Add the mushrooms and cook for 5 to 6 minutes, stirring frequently, or until they are soft and begin to brown.
7. Add the garlic and cook for 1 to 2 minutes, until fragrant.
8. Pour in the warm wine and broth mixture and stir in the pepper, thyme, oregano, and the remaining one teaspoon of salt. Cook for 2 to 3 minutes.
9. Stir in the cream and add the chicken to the skillet, flipping it once to coat. Simmer for 4 to 5 minutes, or until the sauce thickens.
10. Serve on a bed of angel hair pasta garnished with fresh parsley and a lemon wedge for squeezing.
Serving Suggestion: Serve over rice and a side salad.

Variation Tip: Substitute chicken broth with a broth of your choice.
Nutritional Information per Serving:
Calories 960 | Fat 28.5g | Sodium 3932mg | Carbs 24.4g | Fiber 1g | Sugar 3.7g | Protein 87.7g

Pineapple Ginger Chicken Breasts

Prep Time: 10 minutes
Cook Time: 30 minutes
Serves: 2
Ingredients:
• 2 boneless, skinless chicken breasts, rinsed and patted dry
• ½ cup flour
• 1 teaspoon ground ginger
• ½ teaspoon salt
• ¼ teaspoon ground black pepper
• 1½ tablespoons oil
• ⅛ cup soy sauce
• ⅔ cup brown sugar
• 10-ounce can crushed pineapple, drained
• ¼ cup water
Preparation:
1. Mix the flour with the ground ginger, salt, and pepper in a bowl.
2. Dredge the chicken in the flour mixture and shake to remove any excess.
3. Heat the oil in a cast-iron skillet.
4. Add the chicken breasts and cook for 2 to 3 minutes on each side. Remove from the skillet and set aside.
5. Stir in the remaining ingredients in a bowl and pour into the hot skillet.
6. Once the mixture starts to boil, lower the heat to medium-low and return the chicken to the pan.
7. Cook on each side for 12 minutes, or until the center of the chicken is no longer pink.
8. Serve.
Serving Suggestion: Serve over a bed of coconut rice.
Variation Tip: Switch up water with chicken broth.
Nutritional Information per Serving:
Calories 890 | Fat 16g | Sodium 1760mg | Carbs 91.9g | Fiber 3.1g | Sugar 61.2g | Protein 96.2g

Basil Chicken Thighs

Prep Time: 15 minutes
Cook Time: 30 minutes
Serves: 6
Ingredients:
• 1 teaspoon olive oil
• 6 (6-ounce) chicken thighs, skin-on and trimmed
• 1 tablespoon parmesan cheese, grated
• 1 tablespoon dried basil
• 1 garlic clove, minced
• Salt and black pepper, to taste
Preparation:
1. Preheat the oven to 450°F.
2. With your hands, carefully create a pocket between the skin and thigh meat of the chicken things.
3. Add a few drops of oil and remaining ingredients to a bowl and mix until well combined.
4. Stuff the pocket of each thigh evenly with the mixture.
5. In a cast-iron wok, heat the remaining oil over medium-high heat.
6. Place the chicken thighs, skin side down, and cook for about 5 minutes.
7. Carefully flip the thighs and cook for about 10 minutes.
8. Place the wok in the oven and bake for about 20 minutes or until the desired doneness of the chicken.
9. Remove from the oven and set aside for about 10 minutes before serving.
Serving Suggestion: Serve over a bed of white rice.
Variation Tip: You can also use chicken breasts instead of chicken thighs.
Nutritional Information per Serving:
Calories: 334|Fat: 13.1g|Sat Fat: 3.6g|Carbohydrates: 0.2g|Fiber: 0g|Sugar: 0g|Protein: 49.4g

Parmesan Turkey Meatballs

Prep Time: 10 minutes
Cook Time: 15 minutes
Serves: 4
Ingredients:
• 1-pound ground turkey
• 1 egg
• 2 garlic cloves, minced
• Handful fresh sage leaves, minced
• ½ teaspoon sea salt
• ½ teaspoon red pepper flakes
• ½ cup breadcrumbs or panko breadcrumbs
• ¼ cup parmesan cheese, grated
• 4 tablespoons (½ stick) salted butter, divided
• Juice of 1 lemon
Preparation:
1. Preheat the oven to 400°F.
2. Mix the ground turkey, egg, garlic, sage, salt, red pepper flakes, breadcrumbs, and parmesan cheese in a large bowl, ensuring the egg and breadcrumbs are evenly distributed.
3. Form the mixture into 10 to 12 meatballs the size of your palm.
4. In a cast-iron skillet over medium-high heat, melt one tablespoon of butter. Brown the meatballs for 2 to 3 minutes per side, then remove from the heat.
5. Add the remaining three tablespoons of butter to the skillet and squeeze the lemon juice over the meatballs.
6. Bake for 5 to 7 minutes until the meatballs reach an internal temperature of 165°F.
7. Turn the meatballs a few times in the butter before serving.
Serving Suggestion: Garnish with chopped parsley.
Variation Tip: Substitute ground turkey with ground chicken.
Nutritional Information per Serving:
Calories 444 | Fat 29g | Sodium 685mg | Carbs 11.3g | Fiber 0.8g | Sugar 1.3g | Protein 39.1g

Stir-Fried Chicken with Fig Sauce

Prep Time: 15 minutes
Cook Time: 20 minutes
Serves: 4
Ingredients:
• 1½ tablespoons fresh thyme leaves, chopped and divided
• 4 (6-ounce) chicken breast halves, skinless and boneless
• ½ teaspoon salt, divided
• 2 tablespoons olive oil, divided
• ½ cup dried figs, chopped finely
• ¼ cup balsamic vinegar
• ¼ teaspoon ground black pepper

- ¾ cup onion, chopped
- ½ cup chicken broth
- 2 teaspoons low-sodium soy sauce

Preparation:
1. Evenly season the chicken breast halves with 1½ teaspoons of thyme, ¼ teaspoon of salt, and black pepper.
2. In a large-sized cast-iron wok, heat 1 tablespoon of oil and cook the chicken for about 6 minutes on each side over medium-high heat.
3. Put the chicken onto a plate and cover with a piece of foil to keep warm.
4. In the same wok, heat the remaining oil over medium heat and sauté the onion for about 3 minutes.
5. Stir in the broth, figs, vinegar, and soy sauce and simmer for about 3 minutes.
6. Stir in the remaining thyme and salt and remove from the heat.
7. Cut each chicken breast half into long slices diagonally.
8. Serve the chicken slices with the topping of fig sauce.

Serving Suggestions: Serve alongside pasta of your choice.
Variation Tip: You can use turkey instead.
Nutritional Information per Serving:
Calories: 355|Fat: 13.6g|Sat Fat: 2.4g|Carbohydrates: 19.1g|Fiber: 3.3g|Sugar: 13.2g|Protein: 39.9g

Stir-Fried Ground Turkey with Vegetables

Prep Time: 10 minutes
Cook Time: 20 minutes
Serves: 4
Ingredients:
- 1-pound lean ground turkey
- 1 tablespoon olive oil
- 1 large yellow onion, chopped
- 1 (14½-ounce) can diced tomatoes with green chilies
- 1 teaspoon lime juice, freshly squeezed
- 3 cups fresh spinach
- 2 tablespoons taco seasoning
- 1½ cups Mexican cheese blend, shredded

Preparation:
1. Heat the oil over medium heat in a large cast-iron wok and cook the ground turkey for about 8 minutes, breaking it into small crumbles.
2. Add the onion over medium-low heat and cook for about 6 minutes, stirring occasionally.
3. Stir in the tomatoes and taco seasoning and cook for about 2 minutes.

4. Stir in the spinach and lime juice and cook for about 4 minutes.
5. Sprinkle with the cheese and immediately cover the wok.
6. Remove from the heat and set aside, covered, for about 5 minutes before serving.

Serving Suggestions: Serve topped with lime wedges.
Variation Tip: You can also use baby spinach.
Nutritional Information per Serving:
Calories: 259|Fat: 25.1g|Sat Fat: 5.5g|Carbohydrates: 12.8g|Fiber: 2.5g|Sugar: 5.1g|Protein: 32.2g

Homemade Ground Turkey in Marinara Sauce

Prep Time: 10 minutes
Cook Time: 22 minutes
Serves: 3
Ingredients:
- 1 large onion, chopped
- 1 tablespoon extra-virgin olive oil
- 1-pound ground turkey
- 1 tablespoon dried oregano
- 2 cups marinara sauce
- 2 garlic cloves, minced
- 1 teaspoon red pepper flakes, crushed
- 2 tablespoons fresh parsley, chopped

Preparation:
1. In a large-sized cast-iron wok, heat the oil over medium heat and sauté the onion for about 5 minutes.
2. Add the ground turkey, oregano, garlic, and red pepper flakes and cook for about 7 minutes.
3. Drizzle in the marinara sauce and simmer for about 10 minutes.
4. Serve hot with the garnishing of parsley.

Serving Suggestions: Serve over a bed of noodles.
Variation Tip: You can replace fresh parsley with fresh cilantro.
Nutritional Information per Serving:
Calories: 328|Fat: 18.8g|Sat Fat: 4.7g|Carbohydrates: 11.5g|Fiber: 2.7g|Sugar: 5.6g|Protein: 28.1g

Wok-Fried Marinated Lamb Chops

Prep Time: 10 minutes
Cook Time: 6 minutes
Serves: 4
Ingredients:
• 4 garlic cloves, peeled
• 1 teaspoon black mustard seeds, crushed finely
• 1 teaspoon ground ginger
• ½ teaspoon ground cinnamon
• Salt and black pepper, to taste
• 2 teaspoons ground cumin
• 1 teaspoon ground coriander
• 1 tablespoon coconut oil
• 8 medium lamb chops, trimmed
Preparation:
1. Place the garlic cloves onto a cutting board and sprinkle with some salt.
2. With a knife, crush the garlic until a paste forms.
3. In a bowl, blend together the garlic paste and spices.
4. Make 3–4 cuts on both sides of the chops with a knife.
5. Rub the chops generously with the garlic mixture.
6. In a large-sized cast-iron wok, melt the coconut oil over medium heat and cook the chops in it for about 3 minutes per side.
7. Serve hot.
Serving Suggestion: Serve with your favorite salad.
Variation Tip: You can also make this recipe with pork chops.
Nutritional Information per Serving:
Calories: 437|Fat: 17.1g|Sat Fat: 3.3g|Carbohydrates: 2.3g|Fiber: 0.5g|Sugar: 0.1g|Protein: 64.3g

Curry Beef with Veggie

Prep Time: 20 minutes
Cook Time: 25 minutes
Serves: 5
Ingredients:
• 14 ounces' sirloin steak, trimmed and sliced thinly
• 2 teaspoons olive oil
• 3 bell peppers, seeded and cut into 2-inch thin strips
• Salt and black pepper, to taste
• 2 tablespoons red curry paste
• 1-pound fresh green beans, chopped and cut into 2-inch pieces
• ¼ cup water
• 14 ounces plain Greek yogurt, whipped
• 1 cup mango, peeled, pitted, and cubed
Preparation:
1. Evenly season the beef slices with salt and black pepper.
2. Heat the oil over medium-high heat in a large cast-iron wok and cook the beef for about 6 minutes.
3. Place the beef on a plate.
4. In the same wok, add the curry paste over medium heat and sauté for about 1 minute.
5. Add the bell peppers and green beans and cook for about 4 minutes, stirring frequently.
6. Stir in the yogurt and water and bring to a boil.
7. Cover the wok with a lid and cook for about 7 minutes.
8. Stir in the mango and cooked beef and cook for about 3 minutes.
9. Serve hot.
Serving Suggestion: Serve with a drizzle of lemon juice.
Variation Tip: Add spices according to your taste.
Nutritional Information per Serving:
Calories: 314|Fat: 10.1g|Sat Fat: 2.2g|Carbohydrates: 21.2g|Fiber: 4.6g|Sugar: 11.8g|Protein: 34.8g

Herbed Rib-eye Steak

Prep Time: 10 minutes
Cook Time: 6 minutes
Serves: 2
Ingredients:
- 1 rib-eye steak, boneless
- 3 tablespoons butter
- ¼ cup canola oil
- 2 garlic cloves, smashed
- 2 thyme sprigs
- 2 rosemary sprigs
- Salt

Preparation:
1. Heat the oil in a cast-iron skillet over high heat.
2. Season the steak with salt and place it into the skillet. Add the butter, herb, and garlic and sear the steak until lightly browned on both sides or until the steak's internal temperature reaches 145°F.

Serving Suggestion: Serve with mashed potatoes.
Variation Tip: You can add your choice of seasonings.
Nutritional Information Per Serving:
Calories 559 | Fat 55g | Sodium 235mg | Carbs 2.4g | Fiber 0.9g | Sugar 0.1g | Protein 15.9g

Delicious Fried Strip Steak

Prep Time: 10 minutes
Cook Time: 14 minutes
Serves: 4
Ingredients:
- 4 strip steaks
- 3 garlic cloves, crushed
- 3 tablespoons canola oil
- 1 tablespoon fresh thyme
- 2 tablespoons butter
- Pepper
- Salt

Preparation:
1. Season the steaks with salt and pepper.
2. Heat the oil in a cast-iron skillet over medium-high heat.
3. Add the steak to the skillet and cook for 3–4 minutes. Add the garlic and thyme to the top of the steaks.
4. Cover and cook for 8–10 minutes more or until the steaks reach the desired doneness.
Serving Suggestion: Let the steaks cool for 5 minutes, then serve.
Variation Tip: You can use vegetable oil instead of canola oil.
Nutritional Information Per Serving:
Calories 307 | Fat 21.6g | Sodium 136mg | Carbs 1.2g | Fiber 0.3g | Sugar 0g | Protein 26.1g

Simple Juicy Mignon Steak

Prep Time: 10 minutes
Cook Time: 12 minutes
Serves: 2
Ingredients:
- 12 ounces' mignon steaks
- 1 rosemary sprig
- 1 thyme sprig
- 2 tablespoons canola oil
- 1 teaspoon garlic, chopped
- 2 tablespoons butter
- Pepper
- Salt

Preparation:
1. Preheat the oven to 400°F.
2. Heat the oil in a cast-iron skillet over medium-high heat.
3. Season the steaks with salt and pepper, add them to the skillet, and sear for 3 minutes.
4. Turn the steaks and add the thyme, rosemary, garlic, and butter and cook for 3 minutes more.
5. Place the skillet in the preheated oven and bake the stakes for 6 minutes more.
Serving Suggestion: Remove the steaks from the oven and let them cool for 5 minutes, then serve.
Variation Tip: You can add your choice of seasonings.
Nutritional Information Per Serving:
Calories 584 | Fat 41.9g | Sodium 270mg | Carbs 1.2g | Fiber 0.5g | Sugar 0g | Protein 48.9g

Delectable Pork Tenderloin Pieces

Prep Time: 10 minutes
Cook Time: 12 minutes
Serves: 6
Ingredients:
• 2 pounds' pork tenderloin, cut into 1-inch pieces
• 1 tablespoon garlic, minced
• 2 teaspoons honey
• 2 tablespoons canola oil
• 1 teaspoon paprika
• 1 teaspoon Italian seasoning
• Pepper
• Salt
Preparation:
1. In a mixing bowl, mix the meat, garlic, honey, paprika, Italian seasoning, pepper, and salt until well coated.
2. Heat the oil in a cast-iron skillet over medium heat.
3. Add the meat to the skillet and cook for 10–12 minutes or until the internal temperature of the meat reaches 145°F.
Serving Suggestion: Serve with salad or orzo pasta.
Variation Tip: Add your choice of seasonings.
Nutritional Information Per Serving:
Calories 270 | Fat 10.3g | Sodium 114mg | Carbs 2.7g | Fiber 0.2g | Sugar 2g | Protein 39.7g

Skillet-Fried Pork Chops

Prep Time: 10 minutes
Cook Time: 10 minutes
Serves: 4
Ingredients:
• 4 pork chops
• 2 tablespoons canola oil
• ½ teaspoon garlic powder
• ½ teaspoon mustard powder
• 2 teaspoons paprika
• Pepper
• Salt
Preparation:
1. Mix the garlic powder, mustard powder, paprika, pepper, and salt in a small bowl and rub the mixture over the pork chops.
2. Heat the oil in a cast-iron skillet over medium heat.
3. Place the pork chops in the skillet and cook for 4–5 minutes on each side or until the pork's internal temperature reaches 140°F.
Serving Suggestion: Let the chops cool for 5 minutes, then serve.
Variation Tip: Add 1 tablespoon of butter with the oil.
Nutritional Information Per Serving:
Calories 324 | Fat 27.1g | Sodium 95mg | Carbs 1g | Fiber 0.5g | Sugar 0.2g | Protein 18.3g

Garlicky Lamb Chops

Prep Time: 10 minutes
Cook Time: 15 minutes
Serves: 4
Ingredients:
• 8 lamb chops
• 1 tablespoon butter
• 1 tablespoon garlic, minced
• 2 teaspoons dried oregano
• ¼ cup canola oil
• ¼ cup lemon juice
• Pepper
• Salt
Preparation:
1. Add the lamb chops, garlic, oregano, oil, lemon juice, pepper, and salt into a sealable bag and place it in the refrigerator for 2 hours.
2. Melt the butter in a cast-iron skillet over medium heat.
3. Add half the lamb chops into the skillet and cook for 3–4 minutes on each side. Cook the remaining lamb chops.
Serving Suggestion: Sprinkle with more dried oregano and serve.
Variation Tip: You can also use ½ cup fresh oregano Instead of dried oregano.
Nutritional Information Per Serving:
Calories 471 | Fat 29.2g | Sodium 192mg | Carbs 1.5g | Fiber 0.4g | Sugar 0.4g | Protein 48.1g

Palatable Juicy Pork Tenderloin

Prep Time: 10 minutes
Cook Time: 15 minutes
Serves: 4
Ingredients:
• 1-pound pork tenderloin, cut into 2 pieces
• 1 tablespoon canola oil
• 1 teaspoon dried thyme
• ½ teaspoon onion powder
• ½ teaspoon smoked paprika
• 1 teaspoon garlic powder
• 1 teaspoon sweet paprika
• Pepper
• Salt
Preparation:
1. Preheat the oven to 400°F.
2. In a small bowl, mix the sweet paprika, garlic powder, smoked paprika, onion powder, thyme, pepper, and salt and rub the mixture over the pork tenderloin.
3. Heat the oil in a cast-iron skillet over medium heat.
4. Place the pork tenderloin into the skillet and sear for 5 minutes.
5. Place the skillet in the preheated oven and cook the pork for 10 minutes or until its internal temperature reaches 145°F.
Serving Suggestion: Let it cool for 5 minutes, then slice and serve.
Variation Tip: Add a fresh rosemary sprig.
Nutritional Information Per Serving:
Calories 200 | Fat 7.6g | Sodium 104mg | Carbs 1.4g | Fiber 0.5g | Sugar 0.4g | Protein 30g

Fried Cheese Pork Chops

Prep Time: 10 minutes
Cook Time: 15 minutes
Serves: 6
Ingredients:
• 6 pork chops, boneless
• 2 tablespoons butter
• 2 eggs, lightly beaten
• 1 teaspoon garlic powder
• ½ cup parmesan cheese, grated
• 1 cup breadcrumbs
• Pepper
• Salt
Preparation:
1. Preheat the oven to 400°F.
2. Season the pork chops with salt and pepper.
3. Mix the cheese, breadcrumbs, and garlic powder in a shallow dish.
4. Dip each pork chop in the beaten eggs and coat with the cheese mixture.
5. Melt the butter in a cast-iron skillet over medium heat.
6. Place the coated pork chops into the skillet and sear on both sides until lightly golden brown.
7. Place in the preheated oven and bake for 5–10 minutes more.
Serving Suggestion: Allow to cool slightly, then serve.
Variation Tip: You can also use Italian breadcrumbs.
Nutritional Information Per Serving:
Calories 408 | Fat 27.7g | Sodium 332mg | Carbs 13.7g | Fiber 0.9g | Sugar 1.3g | Protein 24.8g

Wok-Cooked Lamb Strips with Pineapple

Prep Time: 10 minutes
Cook Time: 25 minutes
Serves: 4
Ingredients:
• 1-pound boneless lamb shoulder, trimmed and cut into thin strips
• 1 tablespoon olive oil
• Salt and black pepper, as required
• 1 Serrano pepper, seeded and chopped
• 2 cups pineapple, chopped
Preparation:
1. Season the lamb strips with salt and black pepper.
2. Heat the oil over medium heat in a large cast-iron wok and sear the lamb strips for about 5 minutes.
3. Add the Serrano pepper and pineapple and cook for about 6 minutes.
4. Serve hot.
Serving Suggestion: Serve over orzo.
Variation Tip: Add seasonings of your choice.
Nutritional Information per Serving:
Calories: 282|Fat: 11.9g|Sat Fat: 1.2g|Carbohydrates: 10.9g|Fiber: 1.2g|Sugar: 8.2g|Protein: 32.3g

Scrambled Beef Sirloin with Cauliflower

Prep Time: 10 minutes
Cook Time: 12 minutes
Serves: 4
Ingredients:
• 1 tablespoon coconut oil
• 4 garlic cloves, minced
• 1-pound beef sirloin steak, cut into bite-sized pieces
• 3½ cups cauliflower florets
• 3 tablespoons soy sauce
• ¼ cup fresh cilantro, chopped
Preparation:
1. Heat the oil over medium heat in a large cast-iron wok and sauté the garlic for about 1 minute.
2. Add the beef and stir to combine.
3. Increase the heat to medium-high and cook for about 6–8 minutes or until browned on all sides.
4. Meanwhile, add the cauliflower to a pan of boiling water and cook for about 6 minutes.
5. Drain the cauliflower completely.
6. Add the cauliflower and soy sauce to the wok with the beef and cook for about 3 minutes.
Serving Suggestion: Serve with the garnishing of cilantro.
Variation Tip: Coconut oil can be replaced with olive oil.
Nutritional Information per Serving:
Calories: 275|Fat: 10.6g|Sat Fat: 2.7g|Carbohydrates: 6.4g|Fiber: 2.4g|Sugar: 2.4g|Protein: 37.8g

Breaded Pork Tenderloin Slices

Prep Time: 10 minutes
Cook Time: 20 minutes
Serves: 4

Ingredients:
• 1 pork tenderloin, cut into 1-inch-thick slices
• 1 cup all-purpose flour
• 1 teaspoon red pepper flakes, divided
• 1 teaspoon sea salt, divided
• 1 teaspoon garlic powder, divided
• 2 large eggs
• 2 tablespoons apple cider vinegar
• ¼ cup spicy brown mustard
• 1 cup breadcrumbs
• 1 tablespoon olive oil, plus more as needed
• 1 tablespoon salted butter, plus more as needed
Preparation:
1. Pound the pork slices until they're about ¾-inch thick using a meat tenderizer.
2. On a work surface near the stove, set out three small bowls
3. In the first bowl, stir together the flour, ½ teaspoon of red pepper flakes, ½ teaspoon of salt, and ½ teaspoon of garlic powder.
4. Whisk the eggs, vinegar, and mustard in the second bowl.
5. In the third bowl, combine the breadcrumbs with the remaining ½ teaspoon of red pepper flakes, ½ teaspoon of salt, and ½ teaspoon of garlic powder.
6. Dip 3 or 4 medallions into the flour mixture, then the egg mixture, and the breadcrumbs coating all sides of each medallion.
7. Heat the oil and melt the butter in a cast-iron skillet over medium heat.
8. Working in batches, fry the medallions for 2 to 3 minutes per side, then transfer to a rack to drain slightly.
9. Add more butter and oil to the skillet, as needed, between batches.
Serving Suggestion: Serve with fried rice.
Variation Tip: For a milder taste, omit red pepper flakes.
Nutritional Information per Serving:
Calories 469 | Fat 14.4g | Sodium 933mg | Carbs 44.3g | Fiber 2.3g | Sugar 2.2g | Protein 38g

Mustard Lamb Chops

Prep Time: 10 minutes
Cook Time: 20 minutes
Serves: 4
Ingredients:
• 4 lamb chops
• 1 tablespoon canola oil
• ⅓ cup Dijon mustard
• 1 cup white wine

- 1 tablespoon garlic, minced
- ½ ounce fresh thyme
- 2 tablespoons fresh lemon juice
- 2 tablespoons olive oil

Preparation:
1. Add the lamb chops, garlic, thyme, olive oil, lemon juice, pepper, and salt into a sealable bag. Seal it and place it in the refrigerator for 1 hour.
2. Heat the canola oil in a cast-iron skillet over medium heat.
3. Add the lamb chops to the skillet and cook for 4 minutes on each side. Transfer the lamb chops to a plate.
4. Add the white wine to the same skillet and bring it to a boil over medium heat.
5. Add the garlic and mustard, stir well, and cook until the sauce thickens.
6. Return the lamb chops to the skillet and cook over medium-low heat for 2–3 minutes.

Serving Suggestion: Sprinkle with fresh thyme and serve.

Variation Tip: You can add red wine instead of white wine.

Nutritional Information Per Serving:
Calories 327 | Fat 17.9g | Sodium 308mg | Carbs 5.8g | Fiber 2.1g | Sugar 0.9g | Protein 25.3g

Juicy Pork Chops with Onion and Apple

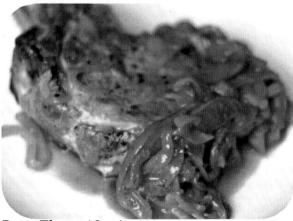

Prep Time: 10 minutes
Cook Time: 20 minutes
Serves: 2
Ingredients:
- 2 pork chops
- ¾ cup chicken broth
- 1 tablespoon Dijon mustard
- ¼ cup white wine vinegar
- 2 fresh thyme sprigs
- 2 tablespoons canola oil
- 1 apple, sliced
- 1 onion, sliced
- Pepper
- Salt

Preparation:
1. Season the pork chops with salt and pepper.
2. Heat the oil in a cast-iron skillet over medium-high heat.
3. Place the pork chops into the skillet and sear for 2–3 minutes on each side. Transfer the pork chops to a plate.

4. Add the apples and onions into the same skillet and cook for 5–6 minutes.
5. Add the thyme, rosemary, salt, and pepper and stir well.
6. Add the broth, mustard, and vinegar and stir well to combine.
7. Return the pork chops to the skillet. Turn the heat to low and simmer for 10 minutes.

Serving Suggestion: Garnish with parsley and serve.

Variation Tip: You can add chicken stock instead of broth.

Nutritional Information Per Serving:
Calories 489 | Fat 35g | Sodium 514mg | Carbs 22.3g | Fiber 4.5g | Sugar 14.4g | Protein 21.2g

Classic Fajitas

Prep Time: 12 hours 10 minutes
Cook Time: 10 minutes
Serves: 4
Ingredients:
- 2 tablespoons olive oil
- Juice of 2 limes
- 2 garlic cloves, minced
- 1 tablespoon chipotle powder
- ½ teaspoon cayenne
- 1 teaspoon ground cumin
- A handful of fresh cilantro, chopped
- 1-pound skirt steak, marinated

For the fajitas:
- 2 tablespoons olive oil, divided
- 1 large yellow onion, sliced
- 1 red bell pepper, cut into ½-inch strips
- 1 green bell pepper, cut into ½-inch strips
- 3 garlic cloves, minced
- ½ teaspoon sea salt

For serving:
- 10 (6-inch) corn tortillas
- Sour cream
- Cilantro
- Lime wedges

Preparation:
1. Combine the olive oil, lime juice, garlic, chipotle, cayenne, cumin, and cilantro in a bowl.
2. Add the steak to the bowl, turning once to coat, then cover and chill for at least one hour or overnight.
3. Heat one tablespoon of olive oil in your cast-iron skillet over medium-high heat. Pat the steak dry.
4. Cook the steak for 2 to 3 minutes, flip, and cook for 2 to 3 more minutes. Remove the steak from the heat and set it aside.

5. Add the remaining olive oil to the skillet with the onion, peppers, and garlic.
6. Cook for 6 to 8 minutes, frequently stirring, until the onion browns. Remove from the heat.
7. Thinly slice the steak and return it to the pan. Season with salt, stir well, and heat for an additional 2 to 3 minutes until sizzling.
8. Serve hot.

Serving Suggestion: Serve with tortillas and sour cream, cilantro, and lime wedges on the side.

Variation Tip: Substitute skirt steak with flank steak.

Nutritional Information per Serving:
Calories 550 | Fat 29.8g | Sodium 383mg | Carbs 37.4g | Fiber 5.8g | Sugar 4.8g | Protein 35.1g

Scrambled Ground Beef with Mushrooms

Prep Time: 15 minutes
Cook Time: 25 minutes
Serves: 4
Ingredients:
• 2 tablespoons olive oil
• 1-pound lean ground beef
• 2 garlic cloves, minced
• 2 cups fresh mushrooms, sliced
• ¼ cup beef broth
• 2 tablespoons fresh parsley, chopped
• ½ of yellow onion, chopped
• 2 tablespoons fresh basil
• 2 tablespoons balsamic vinegar
Preparation:
1. Heat a large-sized cast-iron wok over medium-high heat and cook the ground beef for about 8–10 minutes, breaking up the chunks with a wooden spoon.
2. Transfer the beef to a bowl.
3. In the same wok, add the onion and garlic and cook for about 3 minutes.
4. Add the mushrooms and cook for about 5–7 minutes.
5. Add the cooked beef, basil, broth, and vinegar and bring to a boil.
6. Switch the heat to medium-low and simmer for about 3 minutes.
7. Stir in the parsley and serve immediately.
Serving Suggestion: Serve with your favorite greens.
Variation Tip: You can also use ground turkey.

Nutritional Information per Serving:
Calories: 289|Fat: 14.2g|Sat Fat: 4.2g|Carbohydrates: 3.2g|Fiber: 0.8g|Sugar: 1.3g|Protein: 36g

Roast Beef Tenderloin with Horseradish Sauce

Prep Time: 10 minutes
Cook Time: 30 minutes
Serves: 4
Ingredients:
• 1 beef tenderloin, trimmed of fat
• 2 tablespoons salted butter, room temperature
• 3 garlic cloves, minced
• 1 teaspoon sea salt
• 1 teaspoon crushed black peppercorns
• 1 tablespoon minced fresh rosemary
• 1 tablespoon chopped fresh thyme
• 2 tablespoons olive oil
For the sauce:
• 1 cup Greek yogurt
• ⅓ cup horseradish sauce
• 1 tablespoon spicy brown mustard
• ½ teaspoon sea salt
• 1 teaspoon apple cider vinegar
• 1 tablespoon chives, minced
• 1 tablespoon mayonnaise
Preparation:
1. Heat the oven to 475°F.
2. Mix the butter, garlic, salt, pepper, rosemary, and thyme in a small bowl.
3. Use twine to tie tight circles around the beef in 2-inch intervals to ensure even cooking. Rub the butter and herb mixture all over the beef.
4. Place the prepared tenderloin in your cast-iron skillet and drizzle with olive oil.
5. Roast in the oven for 25 to 30 minutes, until the internal temperature is 125°F.
6. While the beef is roasting, whisk together the yogurt, horseradish, mustard, salt, vinegar, chives, and mayonnaise in a small bowl.
7. Allow the beef to rest for 10 minutes before slicing.
8. Slice into 1-inch rounds and serve warm.
Serving Suggestion: Serve with a huge dollop of horseradish sauce, fresh arugula, and provolone cheese.
Variation Tip: Substitute beef tenderloin with pork tenderloin.
Nutritional Information per Serving:
Calories 218| Fat 17.4g | Sodium 1064mg | Carbs 4.7g | Fiber 0.7g | Sugar 2.3g | Protein 11.5g

Lemony Pork Chops

Prep Time: 10 minutes
Cook Time: 9 minutes
Serves: 4
Ingredients:
• 1 tablespoon Worcestershire sauce
• ½ teaspoon garlic paste
• 2 tablespoons olive oil
• 1 teaspoon lemon juice, freshly squeezed
• Salt and black pepper, as required
• 4 (6-ounce) (½-inch thick) pork chops, boneless
Preparation:
1. Add all the ingredients except for the pork chops to a large-sized bowl and mix well.
2. Add the pork chops and coat them with the mixture generously.
3. Cover the bowl and set it aside at room temperature for about 10–15 minutes.
4. Heat a greased cast-iron wok over medium-high heat and cook the pork chops for about 5 minutes, gently shaking the wok occasionally.
5. Flip the pork chops and switch the heat to low.
6. Cook for about 4 minutes and serve hot.
Serving Suggestion: Serve alongside mashed sweet potatoes.
Variation Tip: You can also use oyster sauce instead of Worcestershire sauce.
Nutritional Information per Serving:
Calories: 308|Fat: 13g|Sat Fat: 4g|Carbohydrates: 0.9g|Fiber: 0g|Sugar: 0.8g|Protein: 44.6g

Pistachio& Garlic-Coated Pork Tenderloin

Prep Time: 15 minutes
Cook Time: 22 minutes

Serves: 4
Ingredients:
• 2 large garlic cloves, peeled
• ⅓ cup shelled pistachios, toasted
• 1-pound pork tenderloin, trimmed
• 1 tablespoon extra-virgin olive oil
• Salt and ground black pepper, as required
• 3 tablespoons orange marmalade
Preparation:
1. Preheat the oven to 450ºF and arrange a rack in the center of the oven.
2. Add the pistachios and garlic to a mini food processor and pulse until finely chopped.
3. Season the pork with salt and black pepper.
4. Heat the oil over medium-high heat in a large cast-iron wok and cook the pork for about 5 minutes.
5. Remove the wok from the heat.
6. Coat the top of pork with the orange marmalade, followed by the pistachio mixture.
7. Transfer the wok into the oven and roast the pork for about 16 minutes.
8. Remove the wok from the oven and place the pork onto a cutting board for about 5 minutes.
9. Cut the pork tenderloin into desired-sized slices and serve.
Serving Suggestion: Serve with a garnishing of parsley.
Variation Tip: You can add more pistachios.
Nutritional Information per Serving:
Calories: 344|Fat: 13.1g|Sat Fat: 1.3g|Carbohydrates: 15.7g|Fiber: 0.9g|Sugar: 12.1g|Protein: 41.1g

Sweet Italian Sausage with Apples

Prep Time: 15 minutes
Cook Time: 30 minutes
Serves: 5
Ingredients:
• 1-pound lady apples, halved through the stem ends
• 1 tablespoon olive oil
• 1½ pounds sweet Italian sausages, pricked
• 2 tablespoons white wine vinegar
• Salt and black pepper, as required
• ¼ cup dry white wine
• 6 cups watercress, trimmed
Preparation:
1. In a large cast-iron wok, heat the oil over medium-high heat.

2. Place the apples in the wok, cut side down, and cook for about 6–8 minutes, flipping occasionally.
3. Add the sausages and cook for about 12 minutes, flipping occasionally.
4. Stir in the wine and vinegar and gently boil.
5. Switch the heat to low and simmer for about 4 minutes.
6. Stir in the watercress, salt, and black pepper and cook for about 2 minutes.
7. Serve hot.
Serving Suggestion: Serve over a bed of rice.
Variation Tip: You can also use dry white wine.
Nutritional Information per Serving:
Calories: 537|Fat: 45.7g|Sat Fat: 6.4g|Carbohydrates: 7.6g|Fiber: 1.6g|Sugar: 4.8g|Protein: 20.7g

Garlicky Lamb Loin Chops

Prep Time: 10 minutes
Cook Time: 12 minutes
Serves: 4
Ingredients:
• 2 pounds' lamb loin chops
• 1 tablespoon butter
• ⅓ cup chicken stock
• ½ teaspoon thyme
• 1 teaspoon fresh lemon juice
• 3 tablespoons canola oil
• 1 tablespoon garlic, grated
• Pepper
• Salt
Preparation:
1. Mix 2 tablespoons of oil, garlic, thyme, lemon juice, pepper, and salt in a small bowl.
2. Rub the lamb chops with the mixture.
3. Heat the remaining 1 tablespoon of oil in a cast-iron skillet over medium-high heat.
4. Add the lamb chops to the skillet and sear for 4–5 minutes on each side. Transfer the lamb chops to a plate.
5. Add the stock to the same skillet and cook for 2 minutes. Add the butter and stir well.
6. Return the lamb chops to the skillet and cook for 4–5 minutes more.
Serving Suggestion: Garnish with parsley and serve.
Variation Tip: You can add chicken broth instead of stock.
Nutritional Information Per Serving:
Calories 545 | Fat 30.1g | Sodium 296mg | Carbs 0.9g | Fiber 0.1g | Sugar 0.1g | Protein 63.9g

Delicious Beef Bourguignon

Prep Time: 10 minutes
Cook Time: 2 hours and 27 minutes
Serves: 4
Ingredients:
• 1 tablespoon vegetable oil
• 6 ounces' bacon, sliced
• 2-pound beef chuck roast, cubed
• 1 large onion, chopped
• ¾ pound carrots, peeled and sliced
• 1 garlic clove, minced
• 12 ounces frozen pearl onions
• 1½ cups beef broth
• 1 teaspoon tomato paste
• ½ teaspoon dried thyme
• ¾ pound mushrooms, sliced
• 3 tablespoons unsalted butter
• 3 tablespoons flour
• Salt and black pepper, to taste
Preparation
1. Preheat the oven to 300℉.
2. In a mixing bowl, combine the butter and three tablespoons of flour.
3. Cook the bacon for 6 minutes in a 9-inch cast-iron pan, then transfer it to a platter.
4. Cook the meat, black pepper, and salt in the same skillet for 5 minutes on each side. Place the steak on a dish.
5. Combine the mushrooms, onions, black pepper, and salt in a mixing bowl.
6. Cook the mixture in the skillet for 10 minutes on low heat.
7. Add the garlic, and cook for 2 minutes.
8. Combine the meat, bacon, carrots, pearl onions, tomato paste, broth, and thyme in a mixing bowl. Place in the skillet and cover.
9. Bake for 2 hours in the preheated oven.
10. Season with salt and pepper to taste.
11. Serve immediately
Serving Suggestion: Garnish with chopped parsley and serve with mashed potatoes
Variation Tip: Switch up dried herbs with fresh herbs
Nutritional Information per Serving:
Calories 472| Fat 30.1g | Sodium 521mg | Carbs 10.8g | Fiber 1.5g | Sugar 4.1g | Protein 27.3g

Seared Pork Chops

Prep Time: 10 minutes
Cook Time: 10 minutes
Serves: 4
Ingredients:
• 4 pork loin chops (1-inch thick)
• ¼ teaspoon Italian seasoning
• Salt and black pepper, to taste
• 2 tablespoons butter
Preparation:
1. Season the pork chops with the salt, pepper, and Italian seasoning.
2. Melt the butter in a 9-inch cast-iron pan over medium-high heat.
3. Cook the pork chops for 5 minutes on each side.
4. Serve immediately.
Serving Suggestion: Garnish with rosemary sprigs.
Variation Tip: Feel free to add in more spices.
Nutritional Information per Serving:
Calories 297 | Fat 24.4g | Sodium 57mg | Carbs 0.4g | Fiber 0g | Sugar 0.3g | Protein 18g

Garlicky Ribeye Steak

Prep Time: 10 minutes
Cook Time: 15 minutes
Serves: 6
Ingredients:
• 2 (12 ounces) ribeye steaks (1¼-inch thick)
• 1 tablespoon vegetable oil
• 1 teaspoon kosher salt
• ¾ teaspoon ground black pepper
• 2 tablespoons butter
• 2 fresh thyme sprigs
• 2 garlic cloves, peeled and crushed
Preparation:

1. Season both sides of the steaks with black pepper and salt.
2. Melt the butter in a 9-inch cast-iron pan over medium-high heat.
3. In a hot cast-iron pan, sear the steaks for 5 minutes on each side.
4. Lower the heat to medium-low and stir in the thyme, garlic, and butter.
5. Grill the steaks for 3 minutes on each side.
6. Serve immediately.
Serving Suggestion: Serve with broccoli.
Variation Tip: Switch up vegetable oil with olive oil.
Nutritional Information per Serving:
Calories 553 | Fat 31.1g | Sodium 415mg | Carbs 2.8g | Fiber 0.1g | Sugar 0g | Protein 31.3g

Honey Pork Chops

Prep Time: 10 minutes
Cook Time: 15 minutes
Serves: 2
Ingredients:
• ¼ cup Dijon mustard
• 1 tablespoon honey
• ½ tablespoon garlic powder
• 2 tablespoons apple cider vinegar
• 2 bone-in pork chops
• ½ teaspoon sea salt
• ½ teaspoon freshly ground black pepper
• 1 tablespoon olive oil
Preparation:
1. Heat the oven to 375°F.
2. Whisk the mustard, honey, garlic powder, and vinegar in a small bowl. Set aside.
3. Pat the pork chops dry and season with salt and pepper on both sides.
4. In your cast-iron skillet, heat the olive oil over medium-high heat.
5. Add the pork chops and sear on both sides for 3 to 4 minutes.
6. Top with the sauce, flipping to coat both sides, and transfer the chops to the oven. Cook for 10 to 12 minutes.
7. Serve hot.
Serving Suggestion: Garnish with chopped parsley.
Variation Tip: For a tangier sauce, drop the honey and double the amount of apple cider vinegar.
Nutritional Information per Serving:
Calories 524 | Fat 34.3g | Sodium 1405mg | Carbs 12.3g | Fiber 1.4g | Sugar 9.5g | Protein 41.8g

Herbed Lamb Chops with Salted Butter

Prep Time: 10 minutes
Cook Time: 15 minutes
Serves: 2
Ingredients:
• 4 lamb chops
• Sea salt, to taste
• 1 teaspoon fresh thyme leaves, minced, plus 1 tablespoon
• 6 tablespoons salted butter, room temperature, divided
• 1 tablespoon fresh rosemary leaves, minced
• 1 tablespoon fresh oregano leaves, minced
• 2 garlic cloves, minced
Preparation:
1. Season the lamb chops with salt to taste and one teaspoon of thyme
2. Let the lamb rest while you make the herb butter.
3. In a small bowl, thoroughly combine four tablespoons of butter, one tablespoon of thyme, the rosemary, oregano, and garlic.
4. In a cast-iron skillet over medium-high heat, melt the remaining two tablespoons of butter.
5. Cook the lamb for 5 to 6 minutes, flip, and cook for 5 to 6 minutes more, or until the internal temperature reaches 145°F. Let the lamb rest for 5 minutes.
6. Serve each chop with a dollop of herb butter on top.
Serving Suggestion: Garnish with parsley.
Variation Tip: Switch up the fresh herbs with dried herbs.
Nutritional Information per Serving:
Calories 705 | Fat 55.1g | Sodium 525mg | Carbs 4.2g | Fiber 2.1g | Sugar 0.2g | Protein 47g

Grilled Pork Quesadillas with Cheese

Prep Time: 10 minutes
Cook Time: 10 minutes
Serves: 4

Ingredients:
• ½ pound barbecued pork, shredded
• 5 green onions, minced
• ½ cup barbecue sauce
• 1 cup cheddar cheese
• ¼ cup fresh cilantro
• 2 tablespoons butter
• 8 flour tortillas (6-inch)
Preparation:
1. Place the barbecued pork in a bowl.
2. Add the barbecue sauce and green onions to the pork. Mix well.
3. Wash and chop the cilantro. Add to the pork. Mix until the ingredients are fully incorporated.
4. Place a 10-inch cast-iron skillet onto the stove and set the heat to medium
5. Butter one side of a whole tortilla. Place it in the skillet and add about 3 to 4 tablespoons to half of the tortilla (more if the tortilla can be filled).
6. Sprinkle 2 to 3 tablespoons of cheese over the pork. Fold the tortilla in half.
7. Grill for about 3 minutes, or until the tortilla is golden brown. Carefully turn the quesadilla.
8. Grill for an additional 2 to 3 minutes; again, cook until the other side is golden brown. Remove from the heat, repeat with the other quesadillas.
9. Serve warm.
Serving Suggestion: Serve with cheesy potatoes.
Variation Tip: Switch up pork with beef or chicken.
Nutritional Information per Serving:
Calories 404 | Fat 18.6g | Sodium 623mg | Carbs 34.5g | Fiber 3.7g | Sugar 9.2g | Protein 25g

Stir-Fried Ground Beef

Prep Time: 10 minutes
Cook Time: 15 minutes
Serves: 4
Ingredients:
• 1 tablespoon vegetable oil
• 1-pound ground beef
• 1 white onion, diced
• 5 garlic cloves, minced
• Sea salt, to taste
• 1 red bell pepper, seeded and thinly sliced
• 1 red chili, seeded and thinly sliced
• 1 carrot, shredded
• 2 tablespoons soy sauce
• 1 tablespoon fish sauce
• Juice of 1 lime
• 2 cups fresh Thai basil leaves

• 2 cups basmati rice, cooked
• 1 scallion, green parts only, roughly chopped
Preparation:
1. Heat the oil in a cast-iron skillet over medium-high heat.
2. Add the ground beef and cook for 2 to 3 minutes, stirring frequently.
3. Add the onion, garlic, and salt and cook for 2 to 3 minutes, frequently stirring, until the beef browns.
4. Stir in bell pepper, red chili, carrot, soy sauce, fish sauce, and lime juice and cook for 2 to 3 minutes.
5. Stir in the basil and cook for 1 to 2 minutes, or until the basil just wilts.
6. Serve.
Serving Suggestion: Serve over rice and topped with scallion greens.
Variation Tip: To make this dish gluten-free, substitute tamari for the soy sauce.
Nutritional Information per Serving:
Calories 705 | Fat 11.3g | Sodium 1431mg | Carbs 100.5g | Fiber 6.9g | Sugar 4.8g | Protein 43g

Spiced Lamb Chops

Prep Time: 10 minutes
Cook Time: 30 minutes
Serves: 2
Ingredients:
• 2 (1¼-inch thick) lamb chops
• 2 garlic cloves, smashed
• 1 tablespoon fresh thyme, chopped finely
• Salt and pepper to taste
• 1½ tablespoons olive oil, divided
• Juice of 1 lime
Preparation:
1. Mix garlic, thyme, salt, pepper, ½ tablespoon oil, and lime juice in a bowl.
2. Mix and rub the lamb chops with this mixture.
3. Preheat the oven to 400℉.
4. Heat the remaining oil in a cast-iron skillet.
5. Add the lamb chops and sear for 3 minutes per side.
6. Transfer the skillet to the oven and cook for 8 to 10 minutes.
7. Remove from the oven and let rest for 10 minutes.
8. Slice and serve.
Serving Suggestion: Serve with scalloped potatoes.
Variation Tip: Feel free to add in more herbs.
Nutritional Information per Serving:
Calories 316 | Fat 21.9g | Sodium 102mg | Carbs 3.7g | Fiber 0.7g | Sugar 0.4g | Protein 27.9g

Rosemary Lamb Chops

Prep Time: 10 minutes
Cook Time: 12 minutes
Serves: 2
Ingredients:
• 2 bone-in lamb chops, excess fat trimmed
• ½ small rosemary sprig, chopped
• 1½ tablespoons olive oil
• 1 garlic clove
• 1 tablespoon French mustard
• ½ tablespoon vinegar
• Salt and pepper to taste
Preparation:
1. Combine the rosemary, half of the oil, mustard, garlic, vinegar, and salt and pepper in a bowl.
2. Add the lamb chops to the bowl and coat well. Marinate in the fridge for 30 minutes.
3. Heat the remaining oil in a cast-iron skillet and add the marinated pork chops.
4. Cook for 6 minutes on each side.
5. Serve.
Serving Suggestion: Serve with a simple salad.
Variation Tip: Switch up the vinegar with lemon juice.
Nutritional Information per Serving:
Calories 433 | Fat 19.5g | Sodium 83mg | Carbs 0.9g | Fiber 0.3g | Sugar 0g | Protein 63.3g

Hoisin Rib-Eye Steak with Sauce

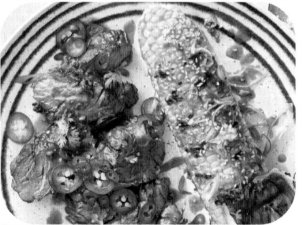

Prep Time: 10 minutes
Cook Time: 10 minutes
Serves: 3
Ingredients:
• 1 (1-pound) (1¼-inch thick) rib-eye steak
• 1 tablespoon canola oil

- Salt and black pepper, to taste
- 3 tablespoons butter
- 1 tablespoon fresh ginger, finely chopped
- 2 tablespoons hoisin sauce

Preparation:
1. Evenly season the steak with salt and black pepper.
2. Heat the oil over medium-high heat in a cast-iron wok and cook the steak for about 3 minutes per side.
3. Stir in the butter, hoisin sauce, and ginger and cook for about 3 minutes, basting the steak with the butter sauce.
4. Transfer the steak to a cutting board.
5. Cut the steak into slices and serve with the pan sauce.

Serving Suggestion: Serve with corn on the cob.
Variation Tip: You can also use ginger paste.
Nutritional Information per Serving:
Calories: 588|Fat: 50.1g|Sat Fat: 9.8g|Carbohydrates: 6g|Fiber: 0.5g|Sugar: 3g|Protein: 27.4g

Beef Stew with Tomatoes

Prep Time: 10 minutes
Cook Time: 1 hour 55 minutes
Serves: 10
Ingredients:
- 3 pounds' boneless beef chuck roast, cut into 1½-inch cube
- 2 onions, chopped
- ¼ cup vegetable oil
- 3 celery stalks, chopped
- 4 garlic cloves, minced
- 1 cup dry red wine
- Salt and black pepper, as required
- 2 (28-ounce) cans Italian-style stewed tomatoes
- ½ cup fresh parsley, chopped

Preparation:
1. In a large-sized cast-iron saucepan, heat the oil over medium-high heat and sear the beef cubes for about 4–5 minutes.
2. Add the celery, onions, and garlic and cook for about 5 minutes, stirring frequently.

3. Stir in the remaining ingredients and gently boil.
4. Switch the heat to low and simmer, covered for about 1 hour 45 minutes.
5. Serve hot.

Serving Suggestion: Serve alongside boiled carrots.
Variation Tip: You can also use dry white wine.
Nutritional Information per Serving:
Calories: 450|Fat: 23.7g|Sat Fat: 5.5g|Carbohydrates: 9.6g|Fiber: 2.6g|Sugar: 5.4g|Protein: 44.1g

Sautéed Ground Pork with Water Chestnuts

Prep Time: 15 minutes
Cook Time: 15 minutes
Serves: 4
Ingredients:
- 1 tablespoon fresh ginger, minced
- 1 tablespoon plus 1 teaspoon coconut oil
- 1 bunch scallion (white and green parts separated), chopped
- Salt, as required
- 1 (18-ounce) can water chestnuts, drained, and chopped
- 2 tablespoons lime juice, freshly squeezed
- 1-pound lean ground pork
- 1 tablespoon 5-spice powder
- 1 tablespoon honey

Preparation:
1. In a large cast-iron wok, melt the coconut oil over high heat and sauté the ginger and scallion whites in it for about 2 minutes.
2. Add the pork and cook for about 8 minutes.
3. Drain the excess fat from the wok.
4. Add the salt and 5-spice powder and cook for about 2–3 minutes.
5. Add the scallion greens and remaining ingredients and cook for about 2 minutes, stirring continuously.
6. Serve hot.

Serving Suggestions: Serve topped with green chilies.
Variation Tip: You can also make this recipe with ground beef.
Nutritional Information per Serving:
Calories: 480|Fat: 21.1g|Sat Fat: 6.4g|Carbohydrates: 50.5g|Fiber: 0.4g|Sugar: 4.5g|Protein: 22.4g

Chicken Alfredo Pasta with Parmesan Cheese

Prep Time: 10 minutes
Cook Time: 25 minutes
Serves: 2
Ingredients:
• ¾ pound boneless, skinless chicken breasts, cut into bite-size pieces
• Salt and pepper, to taste
• 1 tablespoon unsalted butter
• 1 teaspoon garlic, minced
• 2 cups chicken broth
• ½ pound dried penne pasta
• ¾ cups heavy cream, warmed
• ½ cup parmesan, freshly grated, plus extra for serving
• 2 tablespoons fresh parsley leaves, chopped (optional)
Preparation:
1. Melt the butter in a medium-sized cast-iron skillet over medium-high heat.
2. Add the chicken pieces and season with salt and pepper.
3. Cook the chicken until the edges brown while the inside is still pink (about 4 minutes).
4. Transfer to a plate, leaving any brown bits in the skillet, and set aside. Sauté the garlic in the same skillet until fragrant (about 30 seconds).
5. Adjust the flame to high and pour in the broth, scraping any brown bits to loosen.
6. Bring the broth to a simmer and reduce the heat. Let it simmer for 3 minutes.
7. Stir in the pasta and allow it to simmer until tender (about 8 minutes).
8. Stir in the cream and return the chicken, with any juices, to the skillet.
9. Cover and let it simmer until most of the liquid is absorbed and chicken is cooked through (about 4 minutes).
10. Stir in the parmesan and adjust the flavor with seasonings, as desired.
11. Serve with extra parmesan.
Serving Suggestion: Sprinkle with chopped parsley.
Variation Tip: Substitute chicken broth with a broth of your choice.
Nutritional Information per Serving:
Calories 759 | Fat 35.8g | Sodium 1009mg | Carbs 61.6g | Fiber 0.2g | Sugar 1.2g | Protein 46.7g

Walnut Pasta with Mushroom Sauce

Prep Time: 15 minutes
Cook Time: 30 minutes
Serves: 4
Ingredients:
• ⅓ cup extra-virgin olive oil
• 8 ounces' pasta, cooked
• 1 tablespoon butter
• 5 garlic cloves, minced
• 1 teaspoon dried rosemary
• ¼ cup merlot wine
• ½ cup parmesan cheese, grated
• ⅓ cup walnuts, chopped
• 2 shallots, minced
• 24 ounces' fresh mushrooms, sliced
• Salt and black pepper, as required
• 3 tablespoons tomato paste
• ½ cup fresh parsley, chopped
• ¼ teaspoon red pepper flakes
Preparation:
1. In a large-sized cast-iron wok, heat the olive and butter and sauté shallots and garlic for about 3 minutes over medium-high heat.
2. Add the mushrooms, rosemary, salt, and black pepper and cook for about 10 minutes, stirring occasionally.
3. Add the wine, tomato paste, and ¾ cup of water and stir to combine.
4. Switch the heat to medium and cook for about 5 minutes.
5. Add the cooked pasta and toss to combine.
6. Stir in the parmesan cheese, parsley, walnuts, and red pepper flakes and remove from the heat.
7. Serve immediately.
Serving Suggestions: Serve with cheese sticks.
Variation Tip: Walnuts can be replaced with almonds.
Nutritional Information per Serving:
Calories: 585|Fat: 35.8g|Sat Fat: 4.2g|Carbohydrates: 44.3g|Fiber: 3.4g|Sugar: 4.7g|Protein: 27.3g

Creamy Tomato Penne Pasta

Prep Time: 15 minutes
Cook Time: 48 minutes
Serves: 6
Ingredients:
- 2 tablespoons olive oil
- 1-pound penne noodles, cooked and drained
- 4 cloves garlic, minced
- 3 cups marinara sauce
- ½ cup skimmed ricotta
- ¼ cup non-fat, plain Greek yogurt
- ½ cup grape tomatoes, sliced in half
- 1 tablespoon fresh basil, finely chopped
- ½ cup mozzarella cheese, shredded

Preparation:
1. Heat the oil in a large cast-iron skillet and sauté the garlic and grape tomatoes on medium heat for about 5 minutes.
2. Switch the heat to low and add the marinara sauce.
3. Toss all the ingredients together and simmer for about 10 minutes, occasionally stirring.
4. Blend in the Greek yogurt and ricotta.
5. Fold in the cooked penne and toss well.
6. Add the mozzarella cheese and stir well, then serve.

Serving Suggestions: Top with fresh basil before serving.
Variation Tip: You can use any veggie of your choice.
Nutritional Information per Serving:
Calories: 341|Fat: 8g|Sat Fat: 2.9g|Carbohydrates: 54g|Fiber: 4g|Sugar: 8g|Protein: 13g

Bow-Tie Pasta with Asparagus

Prep Time: 15 minutes
Cook Time: 12 minutes
Serves: 6
Ingredients:
- 5 garlic cloves, minced
- ⅛ teaspoon hot pepper sauce
- ¼ cup olive oil
- ½ teaspoon red pepper flakes, crushed
- 1-pound fresh asparagus, cut into 1½-inch pieces
- ½ pound cooked bow-tie pasta, drained
- Salt and ground black pepper, as required
- ¼ cup parmesan cheese, shredded

Preparation:
1. Heat the oil in a large cast-iron skillet. Add the garlic, red pepper flakes, and hot pepper sauce and cook for 1 minute.
2. Add the asparagus, season with salt and pepper, and cook for 8–10 minutes or until the asparagus is tender.
3. Stir in the parmesan cheese.
4. Pour the mixture over the hot cooked pasta and toss to coat.
5. Serve immediately.

Serving Suggestion: Serve topped with fresh basil.
Variation Tip: You can also use mushrooms instead of asparagus.
Nutritional Information per Serving:
Calories: 140|Fat: 5.4g|Sat Fat: 1.9g|Carbohydrates: 20.4g|Fiber: 1.1g|Sugar: 9g|Protein: 4.5g

Easy Tomato Pasta

Prep Time: 10 minutes
Cook Time: 10 minutes
Serves: 4
Ingredients:
- 8 ounces' linguine
- ½ teaspoon red pepper, crushed
- 2 tablespoons canola oil
- ¼ cup basil leaves, chopped
- 1 tablespoon garlic, sliced
- 1 small onion, sliced
- 2 ounces' baby spinach
- 2 cups grape tomatoes, cut in half
- ½ teaspoon salt

Preparation:
1. Add the linguine, basil, garlic, onion, spinach, and tomatoes to a deep cast-iron pan. Drizzle with the oil and season with the crushed pepper and salt.
2. Add 4 cups of hot water and bring the mixture to a boil over medium heat. Cook for 9–10 minutes. Stir occasionally until the liquid is evaporated.

Serving Suggestion: Stir well and serve warm.
Variation Tip: Add 2 ounces of grated parmesan cheese once cooked.
Nutritional Information Per Serving:
Calories 260 | Fat 8.6g | Sodium 323mg | Carbs 38.5g | Fiber 2g | Sugar 3.9g | Protein 8.1g

Sautéed Noodles with Carrots and Bell Pepper

Prep Time: 10 minutes
Cook Time: 20 minutes
Serves: 4
Ingredients:
- 1-pound linguine noodles
- 1 tablespoon honey
- ⅓ cup coconut aminos
- 4 tablespoons peanut butter
- 1 carrot, cut into julienne
- 1 bell pepper, cut into julienne
- ½ teaspoon sesame seeds
- 4 tablespoons green onion, sliced
- 4 tablespoons peanuts, chopped
- 1 teaspoon chili sauce
- 2 garlic cloves, chopped
- 4 tablespoons olive oil

Preparation:
1. Cook the noodles according to the packet instructions. Drain well and set aside.
2. Meanwhile, whisk the coconut aminos, honey, chili sauce, and peanut butter in a medium bowl until well combined. Set aside.
3. Heat the oil in a cast-iron skillet.
4. Add the carrots, garlic, and bell pepper. Sauté for 2–3 minutes.
5. Add the cooked noodles and sauce and toss until well combined.

Serving Suggestion: Sprinkle with green onions, peanuts, and sesame seeds and serve.
Variation Tip: You can add sesame oil instead of olive oil.
Nutritional Information Per Serving:
Calories 374 | Fat 27.1g | Sodium 142mg | Carbs 28.2g | Fiber 3.2g | Sugar 9.1g | Protein 8.8g

Angel Hair Pasta with Tomatoes

Prep Time: 15 minutes
Cook Time: 15 minutes
Serves: 4
Ingredients:

- 2 tablespoons olive oil
- 8 ounces' angel hair pasta, cooked
- 1 tablespoon garlic, minced
- 1 tablespoon dried basil, crushed
- 2 cups cherry tomatoes, halved
- 1 tablespoon dried oregano, crushed
- 1 teaspoon dried thyme, crushed

Preparation:
1. Heat the oil over medium heat in a large cast-iron wok and sauté the garlic for about 1 minute.
2. Stir in the herbs and sauté for about 1 minute more.
3. Add the pasta and cook for about 3 minutes until heated thoroughly.
4. Fold in the tomatoes and remove from heat.
5. Serve hot.

Serving Suggestion: Serve with a topping of parmesan.
Variation Tip: You can use penne pasta in this recipe.
Nutritional Information per Serving:
Calories: 247|Fat: 8.6g|Sat Fat: 1.6g|Carbohydrates: 36.1g|Fiber: 1.7g|Sugar: 2.4g|Protein: 7.5g

Spicy Ramen Noodles

Prep Time: 10 minutes
Cook Time: 10 minutes
Serves: 2
Ingredients:
- 8 ounces fresh ramen noodles
- 1 teaspoon sesame seeds
- 2 tablespoons green onion, sliced
- 2 teaspoons sambal oelek
- 2 tablespoons sesame oil
- Salt

Preparation:
1. Cook the ramen noodles according to packet instructions. Drain well and set aside.
2. Heat the sesame oil in a cast-iron skillet over medium-high heat.
3. Add the sambal oelek and cook for 1 minute.
4. Add the cooked noodles, toss to coat, and season with salt.

Serving Suggestion: Garnish with the green onion and sesame seeds and serve.
Variation Tip: Add your choice of seasonings.
Nutritional Information Per Serving:
Calories 638 | Fat 33.1g | Sodium 2727mg | Carbs 67.6g | Fiber 3.1g | Sugar 0.2g | Protein 13.8g

Spinach Artichoke Lasagna

Prep Time: 10 minutes
Cook Time: 45 minutes
Serves: 6
Ingredients:
• 10 lasagna noodles, broken into 3–4 pieces each
• 10 ounces frozen spinach, chopped
• 10-ounce can artichoke hearts, drained and chopped
• 4-ounce can pimentos, drained and diced
• ½ teaspoon onion powder
• ½ cup parmesan cheese, grated
• ½ cup mozzarella cheese, shredded
• 1 cup water
• 14 ounces Alfredo sauce
• ½ teaspoon garlic powder
• 1 teaspoon dried oregano
• 1 teaspoon dried basil
• 1-pound ground sausage
• 1 tablespoon olive oil
• 3 garlic cloves, sliced
• 1 onion, diced
• ¼ teaspoon pepper
• ¼ teaspoon salt
Preparation:
1. Preheat the oven to 350°F.
2. Heat the oil in a cast-iron Dutch oven over medium-low heat.
3. Add the garlic and onion and sauté for 5 minutes.
4. Add the sausage and cook for 5 minutes.
5. Stir in the basil, oregano, artichoke hearts, pimentos, onion powder, garlic powder, pepper, and salt.
6. Add the spinach and stir well to combine.
7. Add the Alfredo sauce and water and stir well to combine.
8. Add the lasagna noodles, cover, and bake in the oven for 35 minutes.
9. Meanwhile, mix the cheeses.
10. Remove the lid and sprinkle the cheese mixture on top of the lasagna.
11. Return to the oven and cook for 10 minutes more.
Serving Suggestion: Garnish with parsley and serve.
Variation Tip: You can add chicken stock instead of water.
Nutritional Information Per Serving:
Calories 904 | Fat 39.7g | Sodium 4163mg | Carbs 94.6g | Fiber 3.6g | Sugar 2g | Protein 42g

Skillet-Fried Cavatappi Pasta

Prep Time: 15 minutes
Cook Time: 25 minutes
Serves: 8
Ingredients:
• 1 cup yellow onion, chopped
• 1 clove garlic, minced
• 1-pound fresh chorizo sausage, casings removed
• ½ green bell pepper, seeded and chopped
• 1 (10-ounce) can tomatoes with green chilies
• 1 teaspoon taco seasoning
• 1 cup heavy whipping cream
• 1 (15-ounce) can black beans, drained
• 1 (8-ounce) package Monterey Jack cheese, shredded
• 1 teaspoon kosher salt
• 1 teaspoon dried oregano
• 1 cup frozen yellow corn kernels
• 1-pound cavatappi pasta, cooked
Preparation:
1. Cook the chorizo in a 12-inch cast-iron skillet over medium-high heat for 6 minutes or until browned and crumbled.
2. Pour off all except 1 tablespoon of the drippings from the pan.
3. Combine the onion, bell pepper, and garlic in the same skillet.
4. Cook for about 5 minutes, stirring regularly.
5. Cook for 3 minutes after adding the tomatoes, salt, taco seasoning, and oregano.
6. Add the cream, corn, and black beans and allow to boil gently.
7. Remove from the heat and stir in the cooked pasta and cheese.
Serving Suggestions: Serve immediately with a garnishing of lime wedges and fresh cilantro.
Variation Tip: You can also use coconut milk.
Nutritional Information per Serving:
Calories: 602|Fat: 32.5g|Sat Fat: 14.3g|Carbohydrates: 46.4g|Fiber: 10.1g|Sugar: 4.5g|Protein: 32.4g

Scrambled Tofu and Pasta

Prep Time: 15 minutes
Cook Time: 20 minutes
Serves: 6
Ingredients:
For the tofu and pasta:
• 1 (14-ounce) block extra-firm tofu, drained, pressed, and cut into bite-sized chunks
• 1 teaspoon olive oil
• 1 tablespoon plus 1 teaspoon soy sauce
• 1 (12-ounce) package pasta
• ½ teaspoon granulated garlic
For the pesto:
• 2 medium leeks, chopped
• ½ teaspoon olive oil
• 4 cups curly kale, tough ends removed and chopped
• ¼ cup walnuts, toasted and chopped
• 3 teaspoons nutritional yeast
• 6 tablespoons extra-virgin olive oil
• 1 garlic clove, minced
• 3 teaspoons freshly squeezed lemon juice
• ¾ teaspoons salt
Preparation:
1. For the tofu: In a cast-iron wok, heat the oil and cook the tofu, soy sauce, and garlic for about 20 minutes, stirring occasionally, over medium heat.
2. Meanwhile, in a large-sized cast-iron saucepan of boiling water, add the pasta over high heat and cook for about 12 minutes.
3. For the pesto: In a small cast-iron wok, heat ½ teaspoon of oil and sauté the leeks with salt for about 3 minutes over medium heat.
4. Remove the wok from the heat and transfer the leeks into a food processor.
5. Add the remaining ingredients except for the oil and pulse until just combined.
6. While the processor is running, slowly add in the oil and pulse until smooth.
7. Drain the pasta and place into the wok of tofu with the pesto and gently stir to combine.
8. Serve immediately.
Serving Suggestion: Serve topped with black sesame seeds.
Variation Tip: You can use pasta of your choice.
Nutritional Information per Serving:
Calories: 444|Fat: 24.8g|Sat Fat: 4.7|Carbohydrates: 42.9g|Fiber: 2.3g|Sugar: 1.7g|Protein: 17g

Sautéed Rice Noodles with Snow Peas

Prep Time: 15 minutes
Cook Time: 10 minutes
Serves: 2
Ingredients:
For the spicy sauce:
• 1 tablespoon coconut sugar
• 2 garlic cloves, minced
• ½ teaspoon red pepper flakes, crushed
• 2 tablespoons soy sauce
• 2 tablespoons lime juice, freshly squeezed
For the noodles:
• 2 tablespoons sesame oil, toasted and divided
• 6 ounces' thin rice noodles, cooked
• 1 red bell pepper, seeded and thinly sliced
• 12 snow peas
• 1 tablespoon soy sauce
• ¼ yellow onion, sliced thinly
• 4 teaspoons curry powder, divided
For the topping:
• 2 scallions, thinly sliced
Preparation:
1. For the sauce: In a bowl, add all the sauce ingredients and beat until well combined. Set aside.
2. Heat 1 tablespoon of peanut oil in a large cast-iron wok and sauté the bell pepper and onion for about 4 minutes over medium-high heat.
3. Add the snow peas, 2 teaspoons of curry powder, and soy sauce and sauté for about 3 minutes.
4. Put the vegetable mixture into a large-sized bowl.
5. In the same wok, heat the remaining oil over medium heat and cook the noodles, sauce, and remaining curry powder for about 1 minute.
6. Return the vegetable mixture to the wok with the noodles and cook for about 2 minutes, tossing occasionally.
7. Divide the noodle mixture onto serving plates to serve.
Serving Suggestions: Serve topped with chopped scallions.
Variation Tip: You can also use green or yellow bell pepper.
Nutritional Information per Serving:
Calories: 306|Fat: 14.7g|Sat Fat: 2.6g|Carbohydrates: 41g|Fiber: 4.6g|Sugar: 11.3g|Protein: 4.7g

Baked Cheese Penne Pasta

Prep Time: 10 minutes
Cook Time: 25 minutes
Serves: 4
Ingredients:
- 1 pound penne pasta, uncooked
- 24 ounces' marinara sauce
- 14½ ounces Alfredo sauce
- 2 cups mozzarella cheese, shredded

Preparation:
1. Preheat the oven to 350℉.
2. Spray a 12-inch cast-iron skillet lightly with cooking spray.
3. Cook and drain the pasta according to package directions.
4. In the prepared skillet, combine the marinara and Alfredo sauces.
5. Toss in the pasta and thoroughly mix, then top with the cheese.
6. Bake the pasta in a preheated oven for 25 minutes.
7. Serve immediately.

Serving Suggestion: Serve with a cucumber salad.
Variation Tip: Add a pound of ground beef for a varied dish.
Nutritional Information per Serving:
Calories 204 | Fat 5.4g | Sodium 525mg | Carbs 31.7g | Fiber 4.5g | Sugar 5.5g | Protein 7.6g

Chicken Pasta with Tomato Sauce

Prep Time: 10 minutes
Cook Time: 30 minutes
Serves: 4
Ingredients:
- 8 ounces' spaghetti
- 2 tablespoons olive oil
- 8 plum tomatoes, halved and sliced
- 1 teaspoon garlic powder
- ½ teaspoon dried oregano
- 2 tablespoons dried basil
- 1 teaspoon salt
- 1 teaspoon ground black pepper
- 2 garlic cloves, smashed
- 1½ teaspoons white sugar
- 1 tablespoon ketchup
- 3 tablespoons olive oil
- 1 green bell pepper, diced
- 2 boneless chicken breasts, sliced
- 1 red bell pepper, chopped
- 1 red onion, diced
- 1 cup fresh mushrooms, sliced
- ¼ cup grated parmesan cheese

Preparation:
1. Cook the spaghetti as directed on the package, then drain.
2. In a 7-inch cast-iron pan, sauté the tomatoes for 5 minutes with two tablespoons of oil.
3. Combine the ketchup, sugar, black pepper, salt, basil, oregano, and garlic powder in a mixing bowl.
4. Add the chicken to the pan with three tablespoons of oil and cook it for 5 minutes, or until golden brown.
5. Add the garlic cloves and simmer for 1 minute before transferring everything to a platter.
6. Add the mushrooms, onions, red peppers, and green peppers to the same pan.
7. Cook until the onion is tender, add the chicken mixture, and continue to cook for 5 minutes.
8. Combine the pasta and tomato sauce in a large mixing bowl.
9. Serve while still warm.

Serving Suggestion: Garnish with parmesan cheese.
Variation Tip: Substitute the dried herbs with fresh herbs.
Nutritional Information per Serving:
Calories 707 | Fat 13.1g | Sodium 202mg | Carbs 26.2g | Fiber 4.3g | Sugar 10.1g | Protein 25.8g

Spaghetti Carbonara

Prep Time: 10 minutes
Cook Time: 15 minutes
Serves: 4
Ingredients:
- 2 large eggs
- 1 cup parmesan cheese, grated, plus more for serving

- 1 tablespoon olive oil
- 2 tablespoons butter
- 1-pound bacon, cut into 1-inch pieces
- 2 garlic cloves, minced
- 1-pound spaghetti
- 1 teaspoon sea salt
- ½ teaspoon freshly ground black pepper
- ⅓ cup fresh parsley, coarsely chopped

Preparation:

1. In a mixing bowl, whisk together the eggs and parmesan. Set aside.
2. Heat the oil and butter over medium-high heat in a cast-iron skillet.
3. Add the bacon and cook for 8 to 10 minutes, occasionally stirring, until cooked through and browned.
4. Add the garlic to the skillet. While the meat is cooking, boil the pasta in salted water.
5. When the pasta is cooked, strain and reserve ¼ cup of the pasta water. Remove the skillet from the heat and toss the pasta with the bacon, coating it with the drippings.
6. Add the egg mixture and reserved water, stirring quickly to coat the pasta.
7. Plate and top with salt, pepper, parsley, and fresh parmesan.

Serving Suggestion: Serve alongside a salad.
Variation Tip: Add half a pound of spicy sausage to the bacon for an added layer of flavor.
Nutritional Information per Serving:
Calories 959 | Fat 57.5g | Sodium 1639mg | Carbs 64.3g | Fiber 0.3g | Sugar 0.3g | Protein 39.6g

Creamy Tortellini with Sweet Potato

Prep Time: 10 minutes
Cook Time: 20 minutes
Serves: 2
Ingredients:
- 1 tablespoon olive oil
- 1 medium sweet potato, peeled and cut into bite-size cubes
- 2 teaspoons fresh rosemary, minced
- Salt and pepper, to taste
- ¾ cup chicken broth
- 1 bunch spinach, rinsed and torn into bite-size pieces
- ⅓ cup heavy cream
- 2 cups frozen cheese tortellini

Preparation:

1. Heat the oil in a medium-sized cast-iron skillet over medium heat.

2. Add the sweet potato and rosemary, then season with salt and pepper.
3. Cover and cook, with occasional stirring, just until the sweet potato softens (about 5 minutes).
4. Add the broth and scrape any brown bits at the bottom of the skillet.
5. Add the spinach and cook until wilted. Stir in the cream and cover. Bring to a simmer, then add the tortellini.
6. Cook, while frequently stirring, until the tortellini are cooked through (about 10 minutes).
7. Serve while hot.

Serving Suggestion: Serve with garlic bread.
Variation Tip: Substitute heavy cream with half-and-half.
Nutritional Information per Serving:
Calories 401 | Fat 13.2g | Sodium 669mg | Carbs 57.2g | Fiber 7.2g | Sugar 7.7g | Protein 14.6g

Creamy Pumpkin Pasta

Prep Time: 10 minutes
Cook Time: 15 minutes
Serves: 6
Ingredients:
- 12 ounces' pasta
- 2 tablespoons olive oil
- 2 garlic cloves, chopped
- 4½ cups water
- ¼ teaspoon red pepper flakes
- ½ cup parmesan cheese, grated
- 1 cup heavy cream
- 1 cup pumpkin puree
- 2 teaspoons kosher salt

Preparation:

1. Add the pasta, water, garlic, oil, red pepper flakes, pepper, and 2 teaspoons of salt to a cast-iron Dutch oven and stir well. Bring to a boil over high heat.
2. Cook the pasta for 8–10 minutes, then remove from the heat.
3. Add the parmesan cheese, pumpkin puree, and heavy cream, stir well, and season with salt and pepper.

Serving Suggestion: Garnish with parsley and serve.
Variation Tip: You can add chicken or vegetable stock instead of water.
Nutritional Information Per Serving:
Calories 312 | Fat 15.1g | Sodium 875mg | Carbs 35.5g | Fiber 1.2g | Sugar 1.4g | Protein 9.8g

Penne Pasta with Creamy Shrimp

Prep Time: 10 minutes
Cook Time: 18 minutes
Serves: 4
Ingredients:
- 1-pound pasta, penne
- 1-pound raw shrimp, peeled and deveined
- 2 tablespoons butter, melted
- 2 tablespoons flour
- 1½ tablespoons Old Bay Seasoning
- ½ teaspoon salt
- ¼ teaspoon black pepper
- 3 cups milk
- 2 cups mozzarella cheese, shredded
- ½ cup Romano cheese, grated

Preparation:
1. Cook the pasta as directed on the package, then drain. In a 9-inch cast-iron pan, sauté the shrimp in oil for 5 minutes before transferring it to a platter.
2. Combine the butter, flour, black pepper, salt, and Old Bay Seasoning in a cast-iron pan.
3. Add the milk. Cook, constantly whisking, until the mixture slightly thickens.
4. Combine half of the Romano and mozzarella cheeses in a mixing bowl.
5. Add the pasta and shrimp and toss to combine. Mix well, and then sprinkle with the remaining cheese.
6. Broil the pasta for 3 minutes in the oven.
7. Serve.

Serving Suggestion: Garnish with fresh dill.
Variation Tip: Feel free to add in more seasoning.
Nutritional Information per Serving:
Calories 669 | Fat 11.2g | Sodium 713mg | Carbs 49.8g | Fiber 0.1g | Sugar 5.5g | Protein 32.1g

Tomato and Chicken Pasta

Prep Time: 10 minutes
Cook Time: 15 minutes
Serves: 8
Ingredients:
- 1 cup penne pasta, uncooked
- 1 cup parmesan cheese, grated
- ½ cup half and half
- ¾ cup fresh basil, chopped
- 6 tomatoes, chopped
- 1 tablespoon garlic, minced
- 2 tablespoons canola oil
- ½ onion, chopped
- 1-pound boneless chicken breasts, cut in half
- Pepper
- Salt

Preparation:
1. Cook the pasta according to the packet instructions. Drain well and set aside.
2. Heat 1 tablespoon of oil in a cast-iron skillet over medium heat.
3. Place the chicken into the skillet and cook until completely done, about 10 minutes. Transfer the chicken to a plate, then chop.
4. Heat the remaining oil in the same skillet.
5. Add the garlic and onion to the skillet and cook for 5 minutes.
6. Add the basil, tomatoes, and cooked chicken and cook until the basil is wilted.
7. Add the cooked pasta, parmesan cheese, and half and half, and stir until well combined.
8. Turn the heat to high and cook for 5 minutes. Stir constantly.

Serving Suggestion: Stir well and serve hot.
Variation Tip: You can also add Romano cheese instead of parmesan cheese.
Nutritional Information Per Serving:
Calories 262 | Fat 12.4g | Sodium 188mg | Carbs 14.5g | Fiber 1.3g | Sugar 2.8g | Protein 23.3g

Macaroni and Cheese

Prep Time: 10 minutes
Cook Time: 20 minutes
Serves: 2
Ingredients:
- 6 ounces' jumbo elbow macaroni, cooked al dente and drained
- ¾ cup panko breadcrumbs
- ½ teaspoon fresh thyme leaves, coarsely chopped
- 3 tablespoons unsalted butter
- 2 tablespoons all-purpose flour
- 1¼ cups whole milk
- 1¼ cups sharp cheddar cheese, grated
- ¾ teaspoon Dijon mustard

- ⅛ teaspoon kosher salt
- ⅛ teaspoon paprika, or to taste

Preparation:
1. Preheat the oven to 400°F.
2. In a small bowl, mix breadcrumbs and thyme. Set aside.
3. Melt the butter in a cast-iron skillet over medium heat.
4. Scoop out about one tablespoon of the butter, and mix it well into the breadcrumb mixture.
5. Add the flour to the skillet and stir until fragrant (about 1 to 2 minutes). Whisk the roux continuously while adding milk in a thin stream.
6. Use a wooden spoon to continue stirring until the mixture thickens enough to coat the back of the spoon (about 3 minutes).
7. Turn off the heat and stir in the mustard, salt, paprika, and about a handful of cheese.
8. Stir to melt the cheese, adding the rest gradually.
9. Add the cooked pasta and mix to coat evenly with the sauce.
10. Sprinkle with the breadcrumbs.
11. Bake in the oven until the crust is golden brown (about 10 to 15 minutes).

Serving Suggestion: Serve with roasted broccoli.

Variation Tip: Substitute panko breadcrumbs with any other breadcrumbs.

Nutritional Information per Serving:
Calories 669 | Fat 31.2g | Sodium 556mg | Carbs 71.4g | Fiber 6g | Sugar 12g | Protein 24.9g

Ricotta and Sausage Baked Ziti

Prep Time: 10 minutes
Cook Time: 45 minutes
Serves: 4
Ingredients:
- 1-pound ziti or penne pasta, uncooked
- 1 pound ground sweet Italian sausage
- 24 ounces' marinara sauce
- 2½ cups water
- 1-pound fresh ricotta cheese
- 1 fresh mozzarella cheese ball (8 ounces)
- 8 basil leaves, chopped
- 2 tablespoons olive oil
- 2 garlic cloves, minced
- Salt and black pepper, to taste

Preparation:
1. Preheat your oven to 400℉.
2. In a 9-inch cast-iron pan, sauté the garlic with oil for 1 minute over medium heat.
3. Add the ground sausage and simmer for 8 minutes.
4. Season to taste with black pepper and salt.

5. Combine ricotta, basil, water, and marinara sauce in a mixing bowl.
6. Combine all the ingredients in a large mixing bowl, and add the pasta.
7. Bake for 30 minutes, covered with a foil sheet.
8. Remove the foil and top with the mozzarella and ricotta.
9. Preheat the oven to 500℉ and broil the dish.
10. Garnish with basil and serve immediately.

Serving Suggestion: Garnish with grated parmesan cheese.

Variation Tip: Switch up water with your favorite broth.

Nutritional Information per Serving:
Calories 423 | Fat 18g | Sodium 879mg | Carbs 50.9g | Fiber 3.4g | Sugar 6.5g | Protein 15g

Baked Penne Pasta

Prep Time: 15 minutes
Cook Time: 15 minutes
Serves: 8
Ingredients:
- 1 jar (24 ounces) marinara sauce
- 1 pound penne pasta, cooked
- 1 jar (14½ ounces) alfredo sauce
- 2 cups mozzarella cheese, shredded

Preparation:
1. Preheat the oven to 350°F and lightly grease a cast-iron skillet with cooking spray.
2. In a bowl, combine the marinara and alfredo sauces and 1 cup of mozzarella cheese.
3. Add the cooked pasta and toss well.
4. Put the mixture into the skillet and bake in the oven for about 25 minutes.
5. Top with the remaining cheese and bake for another 7 minutes.

Serving Suggestion: Serve with arugula salad.

Variation Tip: You can also add a pound of cooked ground beef or broccoli.

Nutritional Information per Serving:
Calories: 341|Fat: 8g|Sat Fat: 2.2g|Carbohydrates: 54g|Fiber: 4g|Sugar: 8g|Protein: 13g

Creamy Elbow Macaroni and Cheese

Prep Time: 10 minutes
Cook Time: 45 minutes
Serves: 8
Ingredients:
- 1-pound elbow macaroni, cooked and drained
- 2 eggs, lightly beaten
- ½ teaspoon paprika
- ½ teaspoon garlic powder
- 8 ounces' heavy cream
- ½ teaspoon onion powder
- 14 ounces' milk
- 8 ounces' pepper jack cheese, shredded
- 8 ounces' cheddar cheese, shredded
- 1-pound American cheese, shredded
- Pepper
- Salt

Preparation:
1. Preheat the oven to 350°F.
2. Mix the pepper jack cheese, American cheese, and cheddar cheese in a large bowl. Remove ¼ of the cheese mixture from the bowl and set aside.
3. Add the milk, onion powder, cream, garlic powder, paprika, eggs, pepper, and salt into the large bowl of cheese mixture and stir until well combined.
4. Add the cooked macaroni and stir until just combined. Sprinkle over the remaining cheese mixture.
5. Pour the macaroni mixture into a greased cast-iron skillet and bake in the preheated oven for 45 minutes.

Serving Suggestion: Let it cool for 5 minutes, then serve.
Variation Tip: Add your choice of seasonings.
Nutritional Information Per Serving:
Calories 763 | Fat 46.3g | Sodium 1138mg | Carbs 50.8g | Fiber 1.9g | Sugar 8.3g | Protein 35.6g

Cheesy Penne Pasta with Sausage

Prep Time: 10 minutes
Cook Time: 20 minutes
Serves: 4
Ingredients:
- 2½ cups penne pasta, uncooked
- 1 cup pepper jack cheese, shredded
- 1 cup cheddar cheese, shredded
- 1½ cups vegetable stock
- 2 cups crushed tomatoes
- 1-pound sausage, casings removed
- 1 carrot, grated
- 1 teaspoon garlic, minced
- 2 tablespoons canola oil
- 1 medium onion, chopped
- Pepper
- Salt

Preparation:
1. Heat the oil in a cast-iron skillet over medium heat.
2. Add the garlic and onion and sauté until the onion is softened.
3. Add the carrot and sauté for 2 minutes.
4. Add the sausage and cook until completely done.
5. Add the pasta, stock, and tomatoes, stir well, and season with salt and pepper. Bring to a boil.
6. Turn the heat to low and simmer until the pasta is cooked.
7. Remove the skillet from the heat. Add the cheese and cover for 2–3 minutes or until the cheese is melted.

Serving Suggestion: Garnish with parsley and serve.
Variation Tip: You can add chicken stock instead of vegetable stock.
Nutritional Information Per Serving:
Calories 950 | Fat 57.7g | Sodium 1491mg | Carbs 58.8g | Fiber 5.2g | Sugar 9.3g | Protein 47.4g

Baked Rotini Pasta with Parmesan Cream

Prep Time: 10 minutes
Cook Time: 25 minutes
Serves: 2
Ingredients:
• 1 tablespoon unsalted butter
• ¼ pound Italian sausage, removed from casing and crumbled
• Kosher salt and black pepper, to taste
• ½ pound mixed mushrooms, cleaned and thinly sliced
• ½ shallot, finely minced
• ½ teaspoon garlic, minced
• 1½ teaspoons soy sauce
• Juice from ½ lemon
• 4 teaspoons all-purpose flour
• 1 cup chicken stock
• ½ cup heavy cream
• ½ cup parmesan cheese, grated
• 1 tablespoon fresh parsley leaves, chopped
• 1½ teaspoons fresh chives, finely minced
• ¼ pound rotini pasta, cooked al dente according to package instructions and drained
• ½ cup cooking liquid (from pasta)
For the breadcrumb topping:
• ½ cup panko-style breadcrumbs
• ¼ cup grated parmesan cheese
• 1 tablespoon fresh parsley leaves, chopped
• 1½ teaspoons fresh chives, finely minced
• ½ shallot, finely minced
• 1 teaspoon garlic, minced
• 1 tablespoon extra-virgin olive oil
• Kosher salt and black pepper, to taste
Preparation:
1. Combine the ingredients for the topping, mix well, and set aside.
2. Place the butter in a medium-size cast-iron skillet and heat over medium heat.
3. Melt the butter until foaming, then add the sausage. Break the sausage until crumbly and cook until evenly browned.
4. Transfer the crumbled sausage to a plate.
5. Adjust the heat to high and add the mushrooms to the same skillet. Stir-fry until the mushrooms are browned.
6. Add the shallots and garlic and cook, with constant stirring, until fragrant.
7. Stir in the soy sauce and lemon juice.
8. Stir in the flour and cook until the flour forms a film on the bottom of the pan.
9. Gradually add the stock while whisking.
10. Whisk in the cream and simmer until thick. Whisk in the cheese, cooking until melted
11. Stir in the parsley, chives, and sausage. Turn off the heat. Season with salt and pepper.
12. Preheat the broiler. Adjust the oven rack to about 10 inches below the heat source.
13. Add the pre-cooked pasta to the skillet and gradually stir in just enough cooking liquid to separate the pasta without making the mixture soupy.
14. Top evenly with the breadcrumb mixture and place under the broiler until the crust is golden brown (about 2 minutes).
15. Serve hot.
Serving Suggestion: Garnish with chopped parsley.
Variation Tip: Substitute chicken stock with a stock of your choice.
Nutritional Information per Serving:
Calories 536 | Fat 19.4g | Sodium 1654mg | Carbs 68g | Fiber 1.6g | Sugar 1.8g | Protein 29.6g

Chili Chickpeas Stew with Carrot

Prep Time: 15 minutes
Cook Time: 25 minutes
Serves: 4
Ingredients:
• 1 cup onion, chopped
• 2 teaspoons olive oil
• ½ cup carrot, peeled and chopped
• 1 teaspoon garlic, minced
• 1 teaspoon ground ginger
• ⅛ teaspoon ground cinnamon
• ⅛ teaspoon red chili powder
• 2 (15½-ounce) cans chickpeas, rinsed and drained
• 2 tablespoons tomato paste
• 1 tablespoon lemon juice, freshly squeezed
• ¾ cup celery, chopped
• 2 teaspoons ground cumin
• ½ teaspoon ground turmeric
• 2 teaspoons paprika
• Salt and black pepper, as required
• 1 (14½-ounce) can diced tomatoes
• 1½ cups water
• 2 tablespoons fresh cilantro, chopped
Preparation:
1. In a large-sized cast-iron saucepan, heat the oil and sauté the onion, carrot, celery, and garlic for about 5 minutes over medium heat.
2. Add the spices and sauté for about 1 minute.
3. Add the tomatoes, chickpeas, tomato paste, and water and let it reach a gentle boil.
4. Switch the heat to low and simmer, covered, for about 20 minutes.
5. Stir in the lemon juice and cilantro and remove the pan from the heat.
6. Serve hot.
Serving Suggestions: Serve alongside nachos.
Variation Tip: You can also use sweet potatoes in this recipe.
Nutritional Information per Serving:
Calories: 339|Fat: 5.6g|Sat Fat: 0.5g|Carbohydrates: 61.8g|Fiber: 13.2g|Sugar: 6.1g|Protein: 13.2g

Ground Turkey Stew with Pasta

Prep Time: 15 minutes
Cook Time: 40 minutes
Serves: 8
Ingredients:
• 1½ pounds lean ground turkey
• 1 carrot, peeled and chopped
• 1 celery stalk, chopped
• 1 cup tomato sauce
• 1 (14-ounce) can stewed, chopped tomatoes
• 2 teaspoons white sugar
• 3 garlic cloves, minced
• ½ teaspoon dried basil, crushed
• 1 (16-ounce) package dried pasta (of your choice)
Preparation:
1. Heat a little oil in a large-sized cast-iron saucepan and cook the turkey for about 10 minutes over medium heat.
2. Stir in the celery, carrot, tomato sauce, sugar, tomatoes, garlic cloves, and basil and let it reach a gentle boil
3. Switch the heat to low and simmer for about 20 minutes.
4. Meanwhile, in a large-sized saucepan of salted boiling water, add the pasta and cook for about 10 minutes.
5. Drain the pasta well.
6. Add the pasta into the pan with the turkey mixture and cook for about 5 minutes.
7. Serve hot.
Serving Suggestion: Serve with roasted veggies.
Variation Tip: You can use veggies of your choice.
Nutritional Information per Serving:
Calories: 310|Fat: 7.6g|Sat Fat: 0.6g|Carbohydrates: 36.8g|Fiber: 1.3g|Sugar: 4g|Protein: 21.4g

Onion and Fish Stew

Prep Time: 10 minutes.
Cook Time: 35 minutes.
Serves: 3
Ingredients:
• 4 white fish fillets
• ½ teaspoon paprika
• ¼ cup canola oil
• 1 cup water
• 1 onion, sliced
• ¼ teaspoon pepper
• 1 teaspoon salt
Preparation:
1. Add the canola oil, water, paprika, onion, pepper, and salt to a cast-iron pot. Stir well and bring to a boil over medium-high heat.
2. Turn the heat to medium-low and simmer for 15 minutes.
3. Add the fish fillets and cook until they are cooked.
Serving Suggestion: Garnish with parsley and serve.
Variation Tip: Add your choice of seasoning.
Nutritional Information Per Serving:
Calories 530 | Fat 33.7g | Sodium 913mg | Carbs 3.7g | Fiber 1g | Sugar 1.6g | Protein 50.7g

Coconut Onion Pumpkin Soup

Prep Time: 10 minutes
Cook Time: 15 minutes
Serves: 6
Ingredients:
• 2¼ cups pumpkin puree
• 1 tablespoon garlic, minced
• 1 medium onion, diced
• 1 tablespoon butter
• 14-ounce can coconut milk
• 2½ cups chicken stock
• 1 teaspoon curry powder
• Pepper
• Salt
Preparation:
1. Melt the butter in a cast-iron pot over medium heat.
2. Add the onions, garlic, and curry powder and sauté until the onions are softened.
3. Transfer the sautéed onion mixture, stock, and pumpkin puree to a blender and blend until smooth.
4. Pour the blended mixture into the pot and heat over medium heat.
5. Add the coconut milk, stir well, and cook until the soup is warm. Season with salt and pepper.
Serving Suggestion: Garnish with parsley and serve.
Variation Tip: You can also use chicken broth instead of stock.
Nutritional Information Per Serving:
Calories 193 | Fat 16.6g | Sodium 373mg | Carbs 12g | Fiber 3.2g | Sugar 4.1g | Protein 3g

Pork Stew in Tomato Sauce

Prep Time: 10 minutes
Cook Time: 2 hours 20 minutes
Serves: 8
Ingredients:
• 2 pounds' pork belly, sliced
• 3 tablespoons canola oil
• 8-ounce can tomato sauce
• 1 sweet pepper, sliced
• 1½ cups frozen green peas
• 1 tablespoon garlic, minced
• 1 medium onion, minced
• 2 cups chicken stock
• Pepper
• Salt
Preparation:
1. Preheat the oven to 350°F.
2. Heat the oil in a cast-iron Dutch oven over medium heat.
3. Add the garlic and onion and sauté until the onion is softened.
4. Add the meat and cook until it's lightly browned on all sides. Remove the Dutch oven from the heat.
5. Add the stock, sweet pepper, peas, and tomato sauce and stir well.
6. Cover the Dutch oven with a lid, place it in the preheated oven, and bake for 2 hours.
Serving Suggestion: Garnish with parsley and serve.
Variation Tip: You can also add chicken broth instead of stock.
Nutritional Information Per Serving:
Calories 613 | Fat 36.1g | Sodium 2193mg | Carbs 8.4g | Fiber 2.3g | Sugar 4.3g | Protein 54.7g

Cumin Ground Turkey and Veggies Stew

Prep Time: 15 minutes
Cook Time: 45 minutes
Serves: 6
Ingredients:
• 1 red bell pepper, seeded and chopped
• 2 tablespoons olive oil
• 1 onion, chopped
• 1-pound lean ground turkey
• 3 cups tomatoes, chopped finely
• ½ teaspoon ground cinnamon
• 1½ cups frozen corn, thawed
• 2 garlic cloves, chopped
• 2 cups water
• 1 teaspoon ground cumin
• 1 (15-ounce) can red kidney beans, rinsed and drained
• ¼ cup scallion greens, chopped
Preparation:
1. In a large-sized cast-iron saucepan, heat the olive oil and sauté the bell pepper, onion, and garlic for about 5 minutes over medium-low heat.
2. Add the turkey and cook for about 6 minutes, breaking up the chunks with a wooden spoon.
3. Add the water, tomatoes, and spices and let the mixture come to a gentle boil over high heat.
4. Switch the heat to medium-low and stir in the beans and corn.
5. Simmer, covered, for about 30 minutes, stirring occasionally.
Serving Suggestion: Serve hot with the topping of scallion greens, nachos, avocados, and peppers.
Variation Tip: You can also use green bell peppers.
Nutritional Information per Serving:
Calories: 270|Fat: 10.9g|Sat Fat: 3.5g|Carbohydrates: 27g|Fiber: 6.9g|Sugar: 7.2g|Protein: 21.3g

Simple Beef Gumbo

Prep Time: 10 minutes
Cook Time: 20 minutes
Serves: 6
Ingredients:
• 2½ pounds boneless chuck, cut into ¾-inch cubes
• ¾ cup all-purpose flour
• 1½ tablespoons Cajun seasoning
• ½ cup olive oil
• 3 cups yellow onion, chopped
• 2 cups celery, chopped
• 2 cups green bell pepper, chopped
• 4 garlic cloves, minced
• 1 small jalapeño, seeded and chopped
• 6 cups low-sodium beef broth
• 4 dried bay leaves
• 1 teaspoon hot sauce
• 1 tablespoon fresh oregano, chopped
• Fresh oregano leaves, jalapeño slices, for the garnish
Preparation:
1. Flour the beef and season it with the Cajun seasoning.
2. Heat up the oil in a cast-iron wok and cook the beef for about 6 minutes over medium-high heat, stirring regularly.
3. Remove the chicken and drain it on paper towels, reserving the drippings in the wok.
4. Add the onion, celery, bell pepper, garlic, and jalapeño and cook until they're soft, about 5 minutes.
5. Stir in the broth in a slow, steady stream until it's completely smooth. Bring the mixture to a boil with the beef, bay leaves, and spicy sauce.
6. Switch the heat to medium-low, cover, and simmer, turning occasionally, for about 1 hour until the meat is cooked.
7. Toss out the bay leaves. Before serving, add the oregano. If preferred, garnish with oregano and jalapeño.
Serving Suggestions: Serve with hot cooked rice.
Variation Tip: You can also make this gumbo with pork or lamb meat.
Nutritional Information per Serving:
Calories: 671|Fat: 37.9g|Sat Fat: 9g|Carbohydrates: 23.8g|Fiber: 3.3g|Sugar: 5.8g|Protein: 57.4g

Healthy Pork and Veggie Stew

Prep Time: 20 minutes
Cook Time: 1 hour 25 minutes
Serves: 8
Ingredients:
• ¼ cup all-purpose flour
• 3 tablespoons extra-virgin olive oil
• 1 cup shallots, chopped
• 1 cup white wine
• 5 medium carrots, peeled and cut into ¾-inch pieces
• 2 cups chicken broth
• 2½ pounds boneless pork roast, trimmed and cubed
• Salt and black pepper, as required
• 2 small leeks, thinly sliced
• 4 large garlic cloves, minced
• 4 medium potatoes, peeled and cubed
• 1 (18-ounce) can diced tomatoes
• 2 tablespoons balsamic vinegar
• 1 teaspoon dried thyme
• 1 teaspoon dried basil
• ½ cup fresh parsley, chopped
• 2 bay leaves
• 1 teaspoon dried oregano
• 10 ounces cremini mushrooms, cut in half
Preparation:
1. In a medium-sized bowl, add in the pork cubes, flour, ½ teaspoon of salt, and ½ teaspoon of black pepper and toss well.
2. Put the olive oil in a large-sized cast-iron saucepan and cook the pork cubes in two batches for about 3 minutes each over medium-high heat.
3. Shift the browned pork onto a plate.
4. In the same pan, add the leeks, shallots, and garlic and sauté for about 3 minutes.
5. Add in the wine and scrape the browned bits from the bottom.
6. Add the carrots, potatoes, tomatoes, vinegar, broth, bay leaves, thyme, basil, oregano, salt, and black pepper, and let the mixture reach a gentle boil.
7. Switch the heat to low and simmer for about 5 minutes.
8. Stir in the cooked pork and simmer, covered, for about 50 minutes.
9. Add the mushrooms and simmer for about 15 minutes.
10. Serve hot with the garnishing of parsley.
Serving Suggestions: Serve alongside roasted veggies.

Variation Tip: You can add more veggies of your choice.
Nutritional Information per Serving:
Calories: 430|Fat: 11.1g|Sat Fat: 3.3g|Carbohydrates: 34.4g|Fiber: 3.9g|Sugar: 6.1g|Protein: 43.3g

Ground Turkey, Onion and Potato Soup

Prep Time: 15 minutes
Cook Time: 45 minutes
Serves: 8
Ingredients:
• 1 yellow onion, chopped
• 2 tablespoons olive oil
• 2 cups carrots, peeled and chopped
• 2 garlic cloves, minced
• 4 cups tomatoes, crushed finely
• 3½ cups potatoes, cubed
• 8 cups low-sodium chicken broth
• 2 celery stalks, chopped
• 1½ pounds lean ground turkey
• 2 teaspoons red chili powder
• 2 cups sweet potato, peeled and cubed
• Salt and black pepper, as required
Preparation:
1. In a large-sized cast-iron saucepan, heat the olive oil and sauté the onions and carrot for about 3 minutes over medium heat.
2. Add the garlic and sauté for about 1 minute.
3. Add the ground turkey and cook for about 8 minutes, breaking up the chunks with a wooden spoon.
4. Add the tomatoes and chili powder and cook for about 4 more minutes.
5. Add the potatoes and broth and let it reach a gentle boil.
6. Switch the heat to low and cook, covered, for about 25 minutes, stirring occasionally.
7. Stir in the salt and black pepper and serve hot.
Serving Suggestions: Serve as a side dish.
Variation Tip: You can also use vegetable broth.
Nutritional Information per Serving:
Calories: 294|Fat: 10.1g|Sat Fat: 1.4g|Carbohydrates: 29.9g|Fiber: 5.6g|Sugar: 8.4g|Protein: 22.1g

Flavorful Gumbo

Prep Time: 10 minutes
Cook Time: 2 hours
Serves: 6
Ingredients:
• ½ pound thick-cut bacon
• 4 andouille sausages
• 1 boneless, skinless chicken breast
• ½ cup (1 stick) salted butter
• 3 celery stalks with tender greens, chopped
• 1 green bell pepper, seeded and chopped
• 1 white onion, chopped
• 2 garlic cloves, chopped
• 1 cup all-purpose flour
• 2 tablespoons ground paprika
• 1 tablespoon gumbo filé powder
• 1 teaspoon dried oregano
• 1 teaspoon ground coriander
• 1 teaspoon ground cumin
• 1 teaspoon dried thyme
• 1 teaspoon cayenne pepper
• 1 teaspoon red pepper flakes
• 6 cups chicken broth
• 12 okras, thinly sliced
• 1 jalapeño pepper, minced
• 1 teaspoon sea salt
• 5-ounce bottle hot sauce
• 2 pounds' shrimp, peeled and deveined
• 6 eggs
• 5 cups cooked rice
Preparation:
1. In a deep cast-iron pan over medium heat, fry the bacon for 5 to 6 minutes.
2. Remove the bacon using a slotted spoon and leave the grease in the pan.
3. Add the sausages to the pan, and cook for 8 to 10 minutes, occasionally turning, until done. Remove from the pot and set aside.
4. Add the chicken to the pot and cook it for 5 minutes per side. Remove from the pan and set aside.
5. Stir the butter into the bacon drippings.
6. Stir in the celery, bell pepper, and onion. Cook for 3 to 4 minutes until the onion begins to brown.
7. Whisk in the garlic, flour, paprika, gumbo filé powder, oregano, coriander, cumin, thyme, cayenne pepper, and red pepper flakes.
8. Cook for 5 minutes, constantly whisking until the roux browns. While continuing to whisk, slowly pour in the chicken broth. Simmer for 20 minutes.
9. Shred the chicken and slice the sausage. Return the meat to the pan.

10. Stir in the okra and jalapeño pepper, add the sea salt and hot sauce, and stir. Simmer for 1 hour more.
11. Stir in the shrimp. Cook for 4 to 5 minutes until they are opaque.
12. In a medium pot of salted boiling water over high heat, boil the eggs for 6 minutes. Let them cool and then peel (they'll be soft-boiled).
13. In a large soup bowl, serve a generous portion of gumbo over 1 cup of warm rice and top with some crumbled bacon.
Serving Suggestion: Top with deviled eggs.
Variation Tip: For a milder gumbo, omit the cayenne pepper.
Nutritional Information per Serving:
Calories 957 | Fat 51.1g | Sodium 2140mg | Carbs 29.4g | Fiber 3.2g | Sugar 4.3g | Protein 67.1g

Bacon and Bean Stew in Chicken Broth

Prep Time: 10 minutes
Cook Time: 40 minutes
Serves: 4
Ingredients:
• ¼ pound bacon, cut into ½-inch pieces
• 2 cans northern beans, rinsed and drained
• 1 can cannellini beans, rinsed and drained
• 1 can chicken broth
• ¼ cup ketchup
• ½ teaspoon sea salt
• ¼ teaspoon ground black pepper
Preparation:
1. In a deep cast-iron skillet over medium heat, sauté the chopped bacon lightly browned. Remove the bacon and set it aside.
2. Add one can of northern beans and the cannellini beans to the skillet.
3. Pour in the chicken broth, salt, and pepper and let the mixture simmer for 20 minutes.
4. In the meantime, mash the remaining northern beans with a fork and add to the skillet.
5. Add the ketchup and simmer for an additional 20 minutes.
Serving Suggestion: Garnish with chopped parsley.
Variation Tip: Add smoked paprika for a vibrant dish.
Nutritional Information per Serving:
Calories 390 | Fat 13.1g | Sodium 1744mg | Carbs 40.5g | Fiber 14.5g | Sugar 5.9g | Protein 28.1g

Hearty Chili Beans and Tomato Stew

Prep Time: 10 minutes
Cook Time: 1 hour 10 minutes
Serves: 4
Ingredients:
- 1 medium onion, diced
- 1-pound ground beef, browned and drained
- 1 medium can chili beans with seasoning
- 1 can crushed tomatoes
- 1 can diced tomatoes
- 1 teaspoon chili seasoning

Preparation:
1. Place a deep cast-iron pan over medium heat.
2. Add a tablespoon of vegetable oil.
3. Sauté the diced onion until translucent.
4. Add all the remaining ingredients and stir to combine.
5. Cover and simmer for 60 minutes.

Serving Suggestion: Top with shredded cheese and sour cream. Serve hot with cornbread or corn chips.
Variation Tip: Feel free to add in more seasoning.
Nutritional Information per Serving:
Calories 270 | Fat 7.3g | Sodium 253mg | Carbs 11.5g | Fiber 3.3g | Sugar 2.4g | Protein 37.7g

Turkey Culet and Pumpkin Stew

Prep Time: 15 minutes
Cook Time: 50 minutes
Serves: 6
Ingredients:
- 4 large scallions, chopped
- 24 ounces' boneless turkey cutlet, cooked and chopped
- 2 tablespoons canola oil, divided
- 2 teaspoons ginger, finely grated
- 1 cup pumpkin puree
- 1 cup water
- Salt and black pepper, to taste
- 1 (14-ounce) can crushed tomatoes
- 1 teaspoon white sugar
- ¼ cup fresh cilantro, chopped

Preparation:
1. Heat 1 tablespoon of oil in a large cast-iron saucepan and sauté the scallion for about 2 minutes over medium heat.
2. Add the ginger and sauté for about 2 minutes.
3. Move the scallion mixture to a bowl.
4. Put another 1 tablespoon of oil in the same pan and cook the turkey for about 4 minutes over medium heat.
5. Stir in the scallion mixture and remaining ingredients except for the cilantro and gently boil.
6. Switch the heat to low and cook, partially covered, for about 40 minutes.
7. Stir in the cilantro and simmer for about 2 minutes to serve.

Serving Suggestions: Serve with mashed potatoes.
Variation Tip: You can also use leeks instead of scallions.
Nutritional Information per Serving:
Calories: 284|Fat: 10.5g|Sat Fat: 1.9g|Carbohydrates: 10.9g|Fiber: 3.8g|Sugar: 6.1g|Protein: 35.6g

Spinach Tortellini Soup

Prep Time: 10 minutes
Cook Time: 20 minutes
Serves: 6
Ingredients:
- 4 cups baby spinach
- 8 ounces' fresh tortellini
- 14-ounce can white beans, drained and rinsed
- 2 garlic cloves, minced
- 1 small onion, chopped
- 1 tablespoon olive oil
- 4 cups vegetable stock
- ½ teaspoon dried oregano
- 14-ounce can tomatoes, diced
- Pepper
- Salt

Preparation:
1. Heat the oil in a cast-iron Dutch oven over medium-high heat,
2. Add the onion and sauté for 5 minutes. Add the garlic and sauté for 1 minute.

3. Add the tomatoes, stock, and oregano and stir well. Bring to a boil.
4. Once boiling, add the tortellini and cook the pasta according to packet instructions.
5. Once the tortellini is cooked, add the spinach and beans, stir well, and cook for 1 minute.
Serving Suggestion: Top with grated cheese and serve.
Variation Tip: You can add chicken or vegetable broth instead of stock.
Nutritional Information Per Serving:
Calories 233 | Fat 5.9g | Sodium 407mg | Carbs 36.6g | Fiber 6.8g | Sugar 4.6g | Protein 12.2g

Coconut Cayenne Lentil Soup

Prep Time: 10 minutes
Cook Time: 50 minutes
Serves: 8
Ingredients:
- 1 cup red lentils, rinsed
- 14-ounce can tomatoes, crushed
- 1 tablespoon curry powder
- 2 tablespoons canola oil
- 1 teaspoon ginger, grated
- 1 tablespoon garlic, minced
- 10 ounces' spinach, chopped
- ½ cup shredded coconut
- 14-ounce can coconut milk
- ¼ teaspoon cayenne
- 5 cups of water
- 1 onion, chopped
- 2 teaspoons kosher salt
Preparation:
1. Heat the oil in a cast-iron Dutch oven over medium heat.
2. Add the onion and sauté for 6–8 minutes.
3. Add the ginger and garlic and sauté for 4–5 minutes.
4. Add the curry powder and cayenne and stir for 1 minute.
5. Add the lentils, water, shredded coconut, coconut milk, and salt, stir well and bring to a boil.
6. Turn the heat to medium-low and simmer for 25–30 minutes.
7. Add the spinach and tomatoes and cook for 5 minutes.
Serving Suggestion: Garnish with cilantro and serve.
Variation Tip: You can also add almond milk instead of coconut milk.
Nutritional Information Per Serving:
Calories 260 | Fat 16.3g | Sodium 730mg | Carbs 22.7g | Fiber 10g | Sugar 3.3g | Protein 9.2g

Chicken Stew with Gumbo

Prep Time: 15 minutes
Cook Time: 1 hour 45 minutes
Serves: 6
Ingredients:
- 1 pound Cajun sausage, cut into ¼-inch-thick slices
- 1-pound chicken thighs, skinless, bone-in
- ½ cup vegetable oil
- ¾ cup all-purpose flour
- 1 medium onion, chopped
- 1 bell pepper, chopped
- 3 stalks celery, sliced
- 2 tablespoons fresh parsley, chopped
- 2 cups okra, sliced
- 1-quart chicken stock
- 3 cloves garlic, finely diced
- 1 tablespoon Worcestershire sauce
- 14 ounces crushed tomatoes
- 1 tablespoon Creole seasoning
- 1 teaspoon hot sauce
Preparation:
1. Dredge the chicken thighs in flour seasoned with sea salt and pepper.
2. In a large-sized cast iron skillet, heat the oil and sear the chicken, meat side down for 5 minutes over medium-high heat, flipping occasionally.
3. Remove the chicken from the pan; keep aside until needed.
4. Add the peppers, onion, garlic, and celery to the oil and sauté for 1 minute.
5. Add flour to the pan and mix well.
6. Switch the heat to medium heat and allow the roux to cook for about 12 minutes, stirring constantly.
7. Add the chicken stock and mix well until all the roux gets mixed into the stock.
8. Add the Creole seasoning, stewed tomatoes, and Worcestershire sauce and mix well.
9. Switch the heat to low, add the chicken, and simmer, stirring occasionally, for 1 hour.
10. Remove the chicken and allow it to cool.
11. Add the sausage, okra, and chopped parsley to the gumbo. Let it simmer for 30 minutes.
12. Shred the chicken, add it to the gumbo, and simmer it for 5 minutes.
Serving Suggestions: Serve the gumbo over plain white rice.
Variation Tip: You can also make this gumbo with turkey meat.
Nutritional Information per Serving:
Calories: 811|Fat: 54.1g|Sat Fat: 25.4g|Carbohydrates: 43.3g|Fiber: 3.4g|Sugar: 7.2g|Protein: 35g

Tasty White Bean Chili

Prep Time: 10 minutes
Cook Time: 1 hour 30 minutes
Serves: 2
Ingredients:
• ½ pound cannellini beans, soaked overnight, then drained and rinsed
• 1 tablespoon oil
• ½ medium onion, chopped
• ½ teaspoon ground cumin
• 1 garlic clove, minced
• ½ smoked turkey leg, meat removed and chopped
• 3 cups stock
• ½ teaspoon cayenne powder
• ¼ teaspoon chili powder
Preparation:
1. Heat the oil in a deep cast-iron skillet, add the oil and onion, and sauté for 2 minutes.
2. Lower the heat to medium and stir in the garlic and cumin.
3. Cook for 1 minute before adding the turkey meat and the stock.
4. Bring to a simmer before adding beans, cayenne powder, and chili powder.
5. Lower the heat to low and simmer for 75 minutes.
6. Serve and enjoy.
Serving Suggestion: Garnish with parsley.
Variation Tip: For a milder dish, omit cayenne powder.
Nutritional Information per Serving:
Calories 754 | Fat 22.3g | Sodium 1284mg | Carbs 72.9g | Fiber 29.2g | Sugar 4.9g | Protein 66.4g

Chicken and Egg Noodle Soup

Prep Time: 10 minutes
Cook Time: 25 minutes

Serves: 6
Ingredients:
• 1⅓ cup egg noodles
• 2 pounds' chicken, cooked and shredded
• 14 ounces' chicken broth
• 2 garlic cloves, minced
• 1 large onion, diced
• 1 cup celery, diced
• ¼ cup fresh parsley, chopped
• 2 tablespoons canola oil
• 2 teaspoons fresh sage, chopped
• 2 teaspoons fresh rosemary, chopped
• 2 teaspoons fresh thyme, chopped
• 1 cup carrots, diced
• Pepper
• Salt
Preparation:
1. Heat the oil in a cast-iron Dutch oven over medium-high heat.
2. Add the onion, carrots, and celery, and sauté for 5 minutes.
3. Add the garlic and sauté for 1 minute.
4. Stir in the rosemary, thyme, broth, parsley, sage, pepper, and salt, and stir well. Bring to a boil.
5. Turn the heat to medium-low, cover, and simmer for 10 minutes.
6. Add the noodles and stir well.
7. Cover and cook over medium heat for 8 minutes.
8. Add the chicken and cook for 1 minute.
Serving Suggestion: Garnish with more parsley and serve.
Variation Tip: You can also add chicken stock instead of broth.
Nutritional Information Per Serving:
Calories 355 | Fat 10.6g | Sodium 364mg | Carbs 14.9g | Fiber 2.2g | Sugar 2.6g | Protein 47.5g

Creamy Tomato and Carrot Soup

Prep Time: 10 minutes
Cook Time: 20 minutes
Serves: 4
Ingredients:
• 14-ounce can tomatoes, crushed
• 1 carrot, peeled and chopped
• 3 cups chicken broth
• 12 ounces roasted red peppers, chopped
• 2 tablespoons tomato paste
• 1 cup heavy cream
• 2 tablespoons canola oil

- ½ cup fresh basil, chopped
- ½ teaspoon oregano
- 1 tablespoon sugar
- 1 onion, chopped
- 1 teaspoon garlic, minced
- Pepper
- Salt

Preparation:
1. Heat the oil in a cast-iron Dutch oven over medium-high heat.
2. Add the onion, carrot, and garlic and sauté until the onion is softened.
3. Add the tomato paste and stir for 1 minute.
4. Add the red peppers, tomatoes, and broth and stir well.
5. Season with the oregano, sugar, basil, salt, and pepper. Bring to a simmer for 20 minutes.
6. Puree the soup using an immersion blender until smooth.
7. Add the cream and stir well.

Serving Suggestion: Serve with toasted bread.
Variation Tip: You can add your choice of seasonings.
Nutritional Information Per Serving:
Calories 275 | Fat 19.4g | Sodium 1056mg | Carbs 20.8g | Fiber 4.2g | Sugar 13.6g | Protein 6.9g

Carrot and Onion Soup

Prep Time: 10 minutes
Cook Time: 30 minutes
Serves: 6
Ingredients:
- 1-pound carrots, peeled chopped
- 3 tablespoons olive oil
- 1 large yellow onion, wedged
- 1½ tablespoons ginger, grated
- 4 sprigs fresh thyme
- ½ teaspoon ground sage, dried
- ¼ teaspoon nutmeg
- 4 cups vegetable stock
- 2 garlic cloves, minced
- 1 tablespoon pure maple syrup
- 2 bay leaves, dried
- ½ teaspoon salt
- ¼ teaspoon pepper
- ⅔ cup heavy cream

Preparation:
1. Heat the olive oil in a cast-iron wok on the stovetop over medium-low heat.
2. Sauté the carrots for 5 minutes. Add the onions and sauté for an additional 10 minutes.
3. Add all the seasonings and herbs and cook for 2 minutes.

4. Add the vegetable stock and let it reach a gentle boil.
5. Switch the heat to low and simmer for 20 minutes.
6. Remove the thyme stems and bay leaves from the soup.

Serving Suggestions: Top with heavy cream and fresh herbs such as parsley or dill.
Variation Tip: You can also use chicken broth.
Nutritional Information per Serving:
Calories: 117|Fat: 7g|Sat Fat: 1g|Carbohydrates: 13g|Fiber: 3g|Sugar: 7g|Protein: 1g

Skillet-Stewed Chicken Soup

Prep Time: 5 minutes
Cook Time: 45 minutes
Serves: 2
Ingredients:
- 2 chicken thighs, bone-in skin-on
- ¼ teaspoon sea salt
- ¼ teaspoon black pepper
- 1 tablespoon grass-fed butter
- 2 cloves garlic, minced
- ½ onion, finely chopped
- 2 cups chicken bone broth
- ½ cup frozen peas, thawed
- 1 tablespoon parsley, chopped

Preparation:
1. Preheat the oven to 425°F.
2. Season the chicken with salt and pepper.
3. Heat the butter in a large cast-iron skillet and cook the chicken thighs skin-side down for 5 minutes over medium heat.
4. Flip the chicken and cook for 2 more minutes.
5. Divide the onion, garlic, chicken bone broth, and peas evenly between two small cast iron skillets.
6. Add one chicken thigh to each skillet and place in the oven for 30 minutes until the chicken is fully cooked.
7. Garnish with parsley.

Serving Suggestions: Serve with sliced veggies and olives.
Variation Tip: You can add fresh cilantro on top.
Nutritional Information per Serving:
Calories: 452|Fat: 30g|Sat Fat: 10g|Carbohydrates: 8g|Fiber: 1g|Sugar: 1g|Protein: 35g

Chicken Breasts Stew in Beef Soup

Prep Time: 10 minutes
Cook Time: 25 minutes
Serves: 4
Ingredients:
- ½ cup butter, melted
- 6 cups sweet onion, chopped
- 2 tablespoon garlic, minced
- 4 teaspoons fresh thyme leaves, chopped
- ¼ teaspoon salt
- ¼ teaspoon black pepper
- 4 cups beef broth
- 3 chicken breasts, cooked and shredded
- 12 slices (cut into ½-inch cubes) French bread
- 2 cups Swiss cheese, shredded

Preparation:
1. Preheat the oven to 375℉.
2. Melt ¼ cup of butter in a 12-inch cast-iron pan over medium-high heat.
3. After adding the onions, thyme, black pepper, salt, and garlic, cook for 10 minutes.
4. Reduce the heat to medium and continue to simmer for another 10 minutes. Add the chicken and broth and bring the mixture to a boil.
5. Brush the bread with the remaining butter and place it on a cookie sheet.
6. Toast the bread in the oven on both sides for 5 minutes, or until golden brown.
7. Place the bread on top of the cooked soup and serve.
Serving Suggestion: Garnish with parsley.
Variation Tip: Switch up the beef broth with chicken broth.
Nutritional Information per Serving:
Calories 457| Fat 19.6g | Sodium 851mg | Carbs 48.5g | Fiber 4.3g | Sugar 6.7g | Protein 22.5g

Coconut Mushroom Soup

Prep Time: 10 minutes
Cook Time: 20 minutes
Serves: 4
Ingredients:

- 1-pound baby Portobello mushrooms, sliced
- 1 cup yellow onion, chopped
- 1 tablespoon fresh thyme leaves
- 2 tablespoons olive oil
- 4 garlic cloves, minced
- 8 cups vegetable stock
- 13½ ounces canned coconut milk
- 2 tablespoons tamari
- 1 teaspoon fresh lemon juice
- 1 tablespoon vegetable bouillon base
- ¼ cup unbleached all-purpose flour
- ½ teaspoon salt
- ½ teaspoon black pepper

Preparation:
1. In a 15-inch cast-iron pan, sauté the onion, mushrooms, oil, and thyme for 10 minutes.
2. After adding the garlic, cook for 1 minute.
3. Combine the coconut milk, bouillon, tamari, and lemon juice in a medium mixing bowl.
4. Sift the flour over the mushrooms and toss well.
5. Stir in the coconut milk mixture and the broth, and then boil for 10 minutes.
6. Season with black pepper and salt to taste.
7. Serve immediately.
Serving Suggestion: Serve over rice.
Variation Tip: Feel free to use a broth of your choice.
Nutritional Information per Serving:
Calories 349 | Fat 26g | Sodium 1434mg | Carbs 26.2g | Fiber 4.7g | Sugar 6.1g | Protein 8.5g

Herbed Meatball Stew

Prep Time: 10 minutes
Cook Time: 45 minutes
Serves: 4
Ingredients:
- 1-pound ground beef
- 1-pound ground pork
- 1 cup breadcrumbs (freshly made)
- 2 beaten eggs
- ½ cup red onion, chopped
- 2 tablespoons beef bouillon
- 1 teaspoon fresh thyme
- 1 teaspoon black pepper
- 2 tablespoons vegetable oil
- 8 teaspoons flour
- 3 cups water
- 1 packet fried egg noodles
- 4 carrots, sliced
- 1 cup celery, chopped
Preparation:

1. Combine the ground meats, black pepper, ½ teaspoon of thyme, ½ tablespoon of beef bouillon, onion, and eggs in a mixing bowl.
2. Shape the meatball mixture into 32 small meatballs.
3. Heat a 9-inch cast-iron skillet coated with cooking spray over medium heat.
4. Cook for 5 to10 minutes, or until the meatballs are golden brown on both sides. Place the meatballs on a dish. Toss the flour into the drippings and cook until golden.
5. Stir in 4 cups of water, the remaining thyme, and the bouillon.
6. Bring the water to a boil, add the meatballs and vegetables and cook for 35 minutes.
7. Serve immediately.
Serving Suggestion: Garnish with green onions.
Variation Tip: Switch up water with broth.
Nutritional Information per Serving:
Calories 435 | Fat 14.9g | Sodium 264mg | Carbs 23.5g | Fiber 1.7g | Sugar 1.8g | Protein 48.7g

Baby Potato and Beef Stew

Prep Time: 10 minutes
Cook Time: 40 minutes
Serves: 4
Ingredients:
• 1½ pounds boneless stew beef, cubed
• 2 carrots, sliced
• 8 baby potatoes, diced
• 4 cups red wine
• 1½ cups beef broth
• 2 garlic cloves, minced
• 2 tablespoons butter, melted
• 3 tablespoons flour
• ¼ teaspoon salt
• ¼ teaspoon black pepper, ground
• 1 tablespoon olive oil
• 1 teaspoon fresh parsley
Preparation:
1. Preheat the oven to 425℉.
2. In a 9-inch cast-iron pan, combine the potatoes, carrots, black pepper, salt, and olive oil.
3. Bake the veggies in the oven for 20 minutes before transferring them to a platter.

4. Heat 1 tablespoon each of olive oil and butter in the same skillet.
5. Season the meat cubes with black pepper and salt.
6. Sear them for 5 minutes on each side before transferring them to a platter.
7. Stir the flour into the skillet's meat drippings.
8. Cook for 1 minute after adding two minced garlic cloves. Add the wine and beef stock and bring to a boil.
9. Return the veggies and meat to the pan and simmer until the sauce thickens.
10. Serve immediately.
Serving Suggestion: Garnish with parsley.
Variation Tip: For a spicier taste, add red pepper flakes.
Nutritional Information per Serving:
Calories 892 | Fat 15.3g | Sodium 1348mg | Carbs 27.6g | Fiber 6.4g |Sugar 3.4g | Protein 12g

Ratatouille Stew

Prep Time: 10 minutes
Cook Time: 35 minutes
Serves: 4
Ingredients:
• 8 teaspoons olive oil
• 1-pound eggplant, thinly sliced
• 10 ounces' zucchini, sliced
• 1 onion, chopped
• 1 red bell pepper, chopped
• ¾ pound tomatoes, chopped
• 3 garlic cloves, minced
• 1 tablespoon balsamic vinegar
• 3 thyme sprigs
• ½ teaspoon dried oregano
• Salt and black pepper, to taste
• 6 basil leaves
Preparation:
1. Preheat the oven to 400℉.
2. Sauté the eggplant in a 12-inch cast-iron pan with four tablespoons of oil for 5 minutes on each side, or until golden brown.
3. Cook, occasionally stirring, until the zucchini and bell pepper are tender.
4. Stir in the remaining ingredients and bake in the preheated oven for 25 minutes.
5. Serve immediately.
Serving Suggestion: Garnish with parsley.
Variation Tip: Switch up balsamic vinegar with apple cider vinegar.
Nutritional Information per Serving:
Calories 273 | Fat 21.6g | Sodium 53mg | Carbs 17.6g | Fiber 6.8g | Sugar 9.3g | Protein 3.3g

Carrot and Yellow Onion Soup

Prep Time: 10 minutes
Cook Time: 37 minutes
Serves: 3
Ingredients:
- 3 tablespoons olive oil
- 1-pound carrots, peeled and sliced
- 1 large yellow onion, peeled and sliced
- 2 garlic cloves, minced
- 1½ tablespoons ginger, grated
- 1 teaspoon maple syrup
- 4 fresh thyme sprigs
- 2 dried bay leaves
- ½ teaspoon dried sage powder
- ¼ teaspoon salt
- ¼ teaspoon nutmeg
- ¼ teaspoon ground black pepper
- 4 cups veggie broth
- ⅓ cup heavy cream

Preparation:
1. In a 9-inch cast-iron pan, sauté the carrots with the garlic, ginger, onions, and oil for 10 minutes.
2. After adding the herbs and spices, cook for 2 minutes.
3. Add the stock and remaining ingredients and simmer for 20 minutes on low heat.
4. Using an immersion blender, puree the soup and add the cream.
5. Return to the pan and cook for 5 minutes, stirring constantly.
6. Serve while still warm.
Serving Suggestion: Garnish with parsley.
Variation Tip: Feel free to use a broth of your choice.
Nutritional Information per Serving:
Calories 515 | Fat 21.7g | Sodium 813mg | Carbs 36.9g | Fiber 9.6g | Sugar 24g | Protein 2.8g

Kale, Bean, and Potato Stew in Vegetable Soup

Prep Time: 10 minutes
Cook Time: 25 minutes
Serves: 6
Ingredients:
- 3 ounces' kale, chopped
- 14-ounce can black beans, drained and rinsed
- 3 cups sweet potatoes, cubed
- 1 teaspoon cumin
- 1½ teaspoons dried oregano
- 2 tablespoons olive oil
- 1 teaspoon garlic, minced
- 1 large onion, chopped
- 4 cups vegetable broth
- 1 teaspoon garlic powder
- ¼ cup green onion, sliced
- 1 tablespoon fresh lemon juice
- ¼ teaspoon pepper
- ½ teaspoon sea salt

Preparation:
1. Heat the olive oil in a cast-iron Dutch oven over medium-high heat.
2. Add the onion and sauté for 4–5 minutes.
3. Turn the heat to medium. Add the oregano, garlic, garlic powder, cumin, and pepper and sauté for 30 seconds.
4. Stir in the beans, broth, sweet potatoes, and salt and bring to a boil.
5. Turn the heat to low and simmer the soup for 15 minutes.
6. Remove from the heat. Add the kale, green onion, and lime juice and stir well.
Serving Suggestion: Garnish with parsley and serve.
Variation Tip: You can also use soaked and cooked black beans instead of canned beans.
Nutritional Information Per Serving:
Calories 239 | Fat 6.1g | Sodium 925mg | Carbs 38.4g | Fiber 7.3g | Sugar 2.7g | Protein 9g

Delicious Beef and Tomato Stew

Prep Time: 10 minutes
Cook Time: 25 minutes
Serves: 8
Ingredients:
• 15 ounces' beef, cut into pieces
• 4 cups water
• 4 ounces' tomato paste
• 3 tablespoons canola oil
• 12 ounces' okra, cut into pieces
• 1 small onion, chopped
• ¼ cup fresh cilantro, chopped
• 1 tablespoon garlic, minced
• 2 tomatoes, chopped
• Pepper
• Salt
Preparation:
1. Heat the olive oil in a cast-iron pot over medium-high heat.
2. Add the onion, cilantro, and garlic and sauté for a minute.
3. Add the okra, stir well, and cook for 10 minutes.
4. Add the tomato paste, tomatoes, and water and stir well.
5. Add the meat and stir everything well.
6. Turn the heat to low and simmer for 15 minutes., then season with salt and pepper.
Serving Suggestion: Garnish with parsley and serve.
Variation Tip: You can also add chicken stock or broth instead of water.
Nutritional Information Per Serving:
Calories 185 | Fat 8.8g | Sodium 77mg | Carbs 8.3g | Fiber 2.5g | Sugar 3.6g | Protein 18g

Delectable Chicken Stew with Carrot

Prep Time: 10 minutes
Cook Time: 30 minutes
Serves: 8
Ingredients:
• 4 cups chicken, cooked and chopped
• 1 cup white wine
• 3 tablespoons flour
• 3 potatoes, diced
• 1 onion, diced
• 2 cups carrots, sliced
• ½ teaspoon paprika
• 1 teaspoon thyme
• 1 teaspoon garlic
• 5 cups chicken stock
• 1 tablespoon butter
• 1 tablespoon canola oil
• Pepper
• Salt
Preparation:
1. Heat the oil and butter in a cast-iron Dutch oven over medium heat.
2. Add the carrots, potatoes, and onion, season with salt and pepper, and cook until the onion is softened.
3. Sprinkle with the flour and stir well.
4. Add the white wine, stock, thyme, and garlic and stir well. Bring to a boil.
5. Turn the heat to low and simmer for 20 minutes or until the potatoes are cooked through.
6. Add the chicken and cook for 5 minutes more.
Serving Suggestion: Garnish with parsley and serve.
Variation Tip: You can substitute white wine with white wine vinegar.
Nutritional Information Per Serving:
Calories 248 | Fat 5.8g | Sodium 577mg | Carbs 20.3g | Fiber 3.1g | Sugar 3.5g | Protein 22.8g

Spicy Butter-Fried Salmon

Prep Time: 10 minutes
Cook Time: 8 minutes
Serves: 4
Ingredients:
- 2 teaspoons red chili powder
- 2 teaspoons garlic powder
- 2 teaspoons ground cumin
- 2 teaspoons paprika
- Salt and black pepper, as required
- 2 tablespoons butter
- 4 (6-ounce) skinless salmon fillets

Preparation:
1. Mix the spices in a bowl.
2. Coat the salmon fillets evenly with the spice mixture.
3. In a cast-iron wok, melt the butter over medium-high heat and cook the salmon fillets for about 3 minutes.
4. Flip the fish and cook for about 5 minutes until the desired doneness.
5. Serve hot.

Serving Suggestions: Serve with steamed asparagus and boiled rice.
Variation Tip: You can adjust spices according to your taste.
Nutritional Information per Serving:
Calories: 292|Fat: 16.9g|Sat Fat: 7.1|Carbohydrates: 2.8g|Fiber: 1.1g|Sugar: 0.6g|Protein: 33.8g

Lemony and Garlicky Shrimp

Prep Time: 15 minutes
Cook Time: 6 minutes
Serves: 3
Ingredients:
- 3 garlic cloves, sliced
- 2 tablespoons olive oil
- 1-pound shrimp, peeled and deveined
- ½ teaspoon red pepper flakes, crushed
- 1 tablespoon lemon juice, freshly squeezed
- 1 tablespoon fresh rosemary, chopped
- Salt and black pepper, to taste

Preparation:
1. Heat the oil and sauté the garlic slices for about 2 minutes over medium heat in a large-sized cast-iron wok.
2. Transfer the garlic slices to a bowl.
3. In the same wok, add the shrimp, red pepper flakes, rosemary, salt, and black pepper and cook for about 4 minutes, frequently stirring.
4. Stir in the lemon juice, then remove the wok from the heat.
5. Serve hot topped with the garlic slices.

Serving Suggestion: Serve with fresh veggie salad.
Variation Tip: You can also use lime juice.
Nutritional Information per Serving:
Calories: 270|Fat: 12.2g|Sat Fat: 2.3g|Carbohydrates: 4.3g|Fiber: 0.6g|Sugar: 0.2g|Protein: 34.8g

Rosemary Sea Scallops

Prep Time: 15 minutes
Cook Time: 5 minutes
Serves: 3
Ingredients:
- 2 tablespoons fresh rosemary, chopped
- 2 tablespoons olive oil
- 2 garlic cloves, minced
- Pinch of salt
- 1-pound sea scallops
- Black pepper, to taste

Preparation:
1. In a medium-sized cast-iron wok, heat the oil and sauté the rosemary and garlic for about 1 minute over medium-high heat.
2. Add the scallops and cook for about 2 minutes per side.
3. Serve hot.

Serving Suggestions: Serve with fresh rosemary and lemon slices.
Variation Tip: You can also use butter instead of olive oil.
Nutritional Information per Serving:
Calories: 223|Fat: 10.8g|Sat Fat: 1.6g|Carbohydrates: 5.7g|Fiber: 1g|Sugar: 0g|Protein: 25.6g

Garlicky Grouper Fillets

Prep Time: 10 minutes
Cook Time: 15 minutes
Serves: 4
Ingredients:
- 1-pound grouper fillets
- 2 tablespoons Romano cheese, grated
- 1 tablespoon Creole seasoning
- 1 tablespoon garlic, minced
- 3 tablespoons canola oil

Preparation:
1. Preheat the oven to 425°F.
2. Place the fish fillets in a cast-iron skillet.
3. Mix the oil, garlic, Creole seasoning, and cheese in a small bowl.
4. Brush the fish fillets with the mixture.
5. Bake in the preheated oven for 12–15 minutes.

Serving Suggestion: Garnish with parsley and serve.
Variation Tip: You can also add parmesan cheese.
Nutritional Information Per Serving:
Calories 230 | Fat 12g | Sodium 870mg | Carbs 0.7g | Fiber 0g | Sugar 0g | Protein 28g

Blackened Salmon Fillets

Prep Time: 10 minutes
Cook Time: 5 minutes
Serves: 4
Ingredients:
- 1½ pounds salmon fillets
- 1 tablespoon canola oil
- ¼ teaspoon chili powder
- ½ teaspoon onion powder
- ½ teaspoon garlic powder
- 1 teaspoon brown sugar
- 1 teaspoon cumin
- 1 teaspoon paprika
- Pepper
- Salt

Preparation:
1. Mix the paprika, cumin, brown sugar, garlic powder, onion powder, chili powder, pepper, and salt in a small bowl.
2. Season the salmon fillets with the spice mixture.
3. Heat the oil in a cast-iron skillet over medium heat.
4. Place the salmon fillets into the skillet and cook for 2–3 minutes. Turn the fillets and cook them for 2 minutes more.

Serving Suggestion: Garnish with parsley and serve.
Variation Tip: Add 1 lemon wedge to the skillet while cooking the fish fillets.
Nutritional Information Per Serving:
Calories 265 | Fat 14g | Sodium 117mg | Carbs 1.9g | Fiber 0.4g | Sugar 1g | Protein 33g

Butter Shrimp with Red Pepper Flakes

Prep Time: 10 minutes
Cook Time: 10 minutes
Serves: 4
Ingredients:
- 1-pound shrimp, peeled and deveined
- 3 tablespoons fresh lemon juice
- ¼ cup butter
- ½ teaspoon red pepper flakes, crushed
- 1 tablespoon canola oil
- 6 garlic cloves, minced
- Pepper
- Salt

Preparation:
1. Heat the oil in a cast-iron skillet over medium-high heat.
2. Add the red pepper flakes and garlic and sauté for 30 seconds.
3. Add the shrimp, cook for 1 minute, turn the shrimp, and cook for 1 minute more. Season with salt and pepper.
4. Add the butter and lemon juice and cook for 2–3 minutes or until the shrimp is cooked through.

Serving Suggestion: Garnish with parsley and serve.
Variation Tip: You can add your choice of seasonings.
Nutritional Information Per Serving:
Calories 278 | Fat 17g | Sodium 400mg | Carbs 3g | Fiber 0.2g | Sugar 0.3g | Protein 26g

Sautéed Fajita Shrimp

Prep Time: 10 minutes
Cook Time: 5 minutes
Serves: 2
Ingredients:
• 1-pound shrimp, peeled and deveined
• 2 tablespoons butter
• 1 tablespoon fajita seasoning
Preparation:
1. In a bowl, toss the shrimp with the fajita seasoning.
2. Melt the butter in a cast-iron skillet over medium-high heat.
3. Add the shrimp into the skillet and cook for 2–3 minutes. Turn the shrimp and cook for 2 minutes more.
Serving Suggestion: Garnish with parsley and serve.
Variation Tip: You can add your choice of seasonings.
Nutritional Information Per Serving:
Calories 387 | Fat 15g | Sodium 898mg | Carbs 6g | Fiber 0g | Sugar 0g | Protein 51g

Easy-to-Make Garlic Shrimp

Prep Time: 10 minutes
Cook Time: 12 minutes
Serves: 2
Ingredients:
• 1-pound shrimp, peeled and deveined
• 15 garlic cloves, minced
• ½ cup butter
• 1 tablespoon flour
• 1 tablespoon paprika
• Pepper

• Salt
Preparation:
1. Toss the shrimp in the flour, paprika, pepper, and salt in a bowl until well coated.
2. Melt the butter in a cast-iron skillet over low heat.
3. Add the garlic to the skillet and cook for 4 minutes.
4. Turn the heat to medium. Add the shrimp and cook for 2–4 minutes. Turn the shrimp and cook for 2–4 minutes more.
Serving Suggestion: Garnish with fresh parsley and serve.
Variation Tip: Add ¼ teaspoon of cayenne pepper.
Nutritional Information Per Serving:
Calories 734 | Fat 50g | Sodium 963mg | Carbs 15g | Fiber 1.9g | Sugar 0.6g | Protein 54g

Spicy Cod Fillets

Prep Time: 10 minutes
Cook Time: 10 minutes
Serves: 4
Ingredients:
• 4 cod fillets
• 2 tablespoons olive oil
• ½ teaspoon chili powder
• 1 teaspoon brown sugar
• 1 teaspoon cumin
• ½ teaspoon onion powder
• ½ teaspoon garlic powder
• 1 teaspoon paprika
• Pepper
• Salt
Preparation:
5. Mix the paprika, garlic powder, onion powder, cumin, brown sugar, chili powder, pepper, salt, and pepper in a small bowl.
6. Rub the cod fillets with the spice mixture.
7. Heat the oil in a cast-iron skillet over medium heat.
1. Place the cod fillets into the skillet and cook for 4 minutes.
2. Turn the cod fillets and cook for 2–3 minutes more.
Serving Suggestion: Garnish with parsley and serve.
Variation Tip: You can add your choice of seasonings.
Nutritional Information Per Serving:
Calories 160 | Fat 8g | Sodium 124mg | Carbs 2g | Fiber 0.4g | Sugar 1g | Protein 20g

Wok-Fried Salmon with Capers

Prep Time: 10 minutes
Cook Time: 8 minutes
Serves: 4
Ingredients:
• 4 (6-ounce) salmon fillets
• 2 tablespoons olive oil
• 2 tablespoons capers
• 4 lemon wedges
• Salt and black pepper, to taste
Preparation:
1. Heat the oil in a large-sized cast-iron wok and cook the salmon fillets for about 3 minutes over high heat.
2. Sprinkle the salmon fillets with the capers, salt, and black pepper.
3. Turn the salmon fillets and cook for about 5 minutes until browned.
Serving Suggestion: Serve with the garnishing of lemon wedges and dill.
Variation Tip: You can also use cod instead of salmon.
Nutritional Information per Serving:
Calories: 286|Fat: 17.5g|Sat Fat: 7.7g|Carbohydrates: 0.2g|Fiber: 0.1g|Sugar: 0g|Protein: 33.1g

Buttered Tilapia in Chicken Broth

Prep Time: 10 minutes
Cook Time: 8 minutes
Serves: 5
Ingredients:
• 5 (5-ounce) tilapia fillets
• 2 tablespoons unsalted butter
• 3 garlic cloves, minced
• 3 tablespoons homemade chicken broth
• 1 tablespoon fresh ginger, minced

• Salt and black pepper, as required
Preparation:
1. Put the butter in a large-sized cast-iron wok and cook the tilapia fillets for about 3 minutes over medium heat.
2. Flip the fillets over and stir in the garlic and ginger.
3. Cook for about 2 minutes.
4. Add the broth and cook for about 3 more minutes.
5. Remove from the heat and serve hot.
Serving Suggestions: Serve with a topping of roasted lemons and chives.
Variation Tip: You can use dry red wine.
Nutritional Information per Serving:
Calories: 162|Fat: 5.9g|Sat Fat: 0.5g|Carbohydrates: 0.8g|Fiber: 0.1g|Sugar: 0.1g|Protein: 26.7g

Palatable Tuna Patties

Prep Time: 10 minutes
Cook Time: 10 minutes
Serves: 5
Ingredients:
• 1½ cans tuna, drained
• 1 tablespoon canola oil
• ¼ teaspoon dried herbs
• ¼ teaspoon garlic powder
• 1½ tablespoons onion, minced
• 1 celery stalk, chopped
• 1½ tablespoons Romano cheese, grated
• ¼ cup breadcrumbs
• ½ tablespoon lemon juice
• ½ lemon zest
• 1 egg, lightly beaten
• Pepper
• Salt
Preparation:
1. Add the tuna and remaining ingredients to a mixing bowl and mix until well combined.
2. Make equal-shaped patties from the tuna mixture and place them onto a plate. Place the patties in the refrigerator for 1 hour.
3. Heat the oil in a cast-iron skillet over medium heat.
4. Place the tuna patties into the skillet and cook for 5 minutes on each side.
Serving Suggestion: Garnish with parsley and serve with a sauce of your choice.
Variation Tip: You can add crushed crackers instead of breadcrumbs.
Nutritional Information Per Serving:
Calories 164 | Fat 8g | Sodium 113mg | Carbs 5g | Fiber 0.6g | Sugar 1g | Protein 16g

Seasoned Tilapia Fillet

Prep Time: 10 minutes
Cook Time: 8 minutes
Serves: 4
Ingredients:
• 2 tablespoons BBQ seasoning
• 2 teaspoons olive oil
• 4 (5-ounce) tilapia fillets
• Salt and black pepper, as required
Preparation:
1. Season each tilapia fillet with BBQ seasoning, salt, and black pepper.
2. In a cast-iron saucepan, heat the oil and cook the tilapia fillets for about 4 minutes per side over medium-high heat.
3. Put the tilapia fillets onto serving plates.
4. Serve hot.
Serving Suggestion: Serve with roasted asparagus.
Variation Tip: You can use seasonings of your choice.
Nutritional Information per Serving:
Calories: 142|Fat: 3.7g|Sat Fat: 0.9g|Carbohydrates: 0.7g|Fiber: 0.2g|Sugar: 0.2g|Protein: 26.8g

Sesame Seed-Coated Tuna Steaks

Prep Time: 10 minutes
Cook Time: 3 minutes
Serves: 2
Ingredients:
• 2 (4-ounce) ahi tuna steaks
• 1 tablespoon vegetable oil
• 4 tablespoons sesame seeds
• Salt and black pepper, to taste
Preparation:
1. Rub the tuna steaks evenly with salt and black pepper.
2. Place the sesame seeds onto a shallow plate.

3. Gently press the tuna steaks into the seeds to coat evenly.
4. In a medium-sized cast-iron wok, heat the oil and sear the tuna for about 1 minute per side over medium-high heat.
5. Put the tuna steaks onto a cutting board.
6. Cut each tuna steak into desired-sized slices and serve.
Serving Suggestions: Serve with broccoli and rice.
Variation Tip: You can use either white or black (or both!) sesame seeds.
Nutritional Information per Serving:
Calories: 372|Fat: 22.9g|Sat Fat: 7.9g|Carbohydrates: 4.2g|Fiber: 2.1g|Sugar: 0.1g|Protein: 37.1g

Flavorful Crab Cakes

Prep Time: 10 minutes
Cook Time: 6 minutes
Serves: 6
Ingredients:
• 1 egg, lightly beaten
• 2 tablespoons olive oil
• ¼ cup breadcrumbs
• ½ pound lump crab meat
• ¼ cup scallions, chopped
• 1 tablespoon parsley, chopped
• 1 teaspoon Worcestershire sauce
• ¼ teaspoon red pepper flakes
• ½ teaspoon Dijon mustard
• 1½ tablespoons mayonnaise
• ½ cup crushed crackers
• ¼ cup celery, chopped
• Pepper
• Salt
Preparation:
1. In a bowl, add the crab meat and remaining ingredients except for the breadcrumbs and mix until well combined.
2. Make equal-shaped patties from the crab meat mixture and coat them with the breadcrumbs.
3. Heat the oil in a cast-iron skillet over medium heat.
4. Place the crab patties into the skillet and cook for 2–3 minutes on each side.
Serving Suggestion: Garnish with parsley and serve with a sauce of your choice.
Variation Tip: Add ½ teaspoon of Old Bay Seasoning.
Nutritional Information Per Serving:
Calories 114 | Fat 10g | Sodium 328mg | Carbs 5g | Fiber 0.4g | Sugar 0.9g | Protein 7g

Seared Squid Rings

Prep Time: 10 minutes
Cook Time: 13 minutes
Serves: 2
Ingredients:
• ¼ yellow onion, sliced
• ¼ teaspoon ground turmeric
• 1 teaspoon olive oil
• 1-pound squid, sliced into rings
• Salt, to taste
• 1 egg, beaten
Preparation:
1. In a cast-iron wok, heat the oil and sauté the onion for about 5 minutes over medium-high heat.
2. Add the squid rings, turmeric, and salt and toss to coat well.
3. Switch the heat to medium-low and simmer for about 5 minutes.
4. Add the beaten egg and cook for about 3 minutes, stirring continuously.
5. Serve hot.
Serving Suggestion: Serve topped with fresh coriander.
Variation Tip: You can use seafood of your choice.
Nutritional Information per Serving:
Calories: 267|Fat: 7.7g|Sat Fat: 1.9g|Carbohydrates: 8.6g|Fiber: 0.8g|Sugar: 0.8g|Protein: 38.3g

Lemon Honey Salmon

Prep Time: 10 minutes
Cook Time: 12 minutes
Serves: 4
Ingredients:
• 1-pound salmon fillets
• 1 tablespoon garlic, minced
• ¼ cup honey
• 1 tablespoon soy sauce
• 1 tablespoon canola oil
• 1 tablespoon lemon juice
• Pepper

• Salt
Preparation:
1. Heat the oil in a cast-iron skillet over medium-high heat.
2. Season the salmon with salt and pepper, place it in the skillet, and cook for 4–5 minutes or until cooked through.
3. Meanwhile, mix the honey, soy sauce, lemon juice, and garlic in a small bowl.
4. Remove the salmon fillets from the skillet and set them aside.
5. Pour the honey mixture into the skillet and cook until thickened.
6. Return the fish fillets into the skillet and spoon the honey mixture over the fish fillets.
Serving Suggestion: Drizzle with lemon juice and serve.
Variation Tip: You can also add liquid aminos instead of soy sauce.
Nutritional Information Per Serving:
Calories 252 | Fat 10g | Sodium 316mg | Carbs 18g | Fiber 0.1g | Sugar 17g | Protein 22g

Thyme Scallops

Prep Time: 10 minutes
Cook Time: 10 minutes
Serves: 4
Ingredients:
• 12 sea scallops
• 2 thyme sprigs
• ¼ cup butter
• 2 tablespoons canola oil
• ¼ cup lemon juice
• Pepper
• Salt
Preparation:
1. Season the scallops with salt and pepper.
2. Heat the oil in a cast-iron skillet over medium-high heat for 5 minutes.
3. Add the scallops and sear for 2–3 minutes. Turn the scallops and cook for 1–2 minutes.
4. Remove the scallops from the skillet.
5. Melt the butter in the same skillet and allow it to brown for 2 minutes.
6. Add the lemon juice and thyme and stir well. Pour the butter mixture over the scallops and serve.
Serving Suggestion: Garnish the scallops with freshly chopped parsley.
Variation Tip: Add your choice of seasonings.
Nutritional Information Per Serving:
Calories 247 | Fat 19g | Sodium 268mg | Carbs 2g | Fiber 0.1g | Sugar 0.3g | Protein 15g

Lemony Anise Salmon

Prep Time: 10 minutes
Cook Time: 15 minutes
Serves: 2
Ingredients:
- 2 salmon fillets, filleted
- ⅛ cup orange juice
- ¼ cup lemon juice
- 1-star anise piece
- ½ teaspoon honey
- ½ tablespoon vegetable oil
- ½ teaspoon cornflour
- Salt and pepper, to taste

Preparation:
1. Combine the orange juice, lemon juice, star anise, and honey in a bowl. Season with salt and pepper and add the salmon fillets. Marinate in the fridge for 30 minutes.
2. Heat the oil in a cast-iron skillet. Add the salmon fillets with some of the marinade and cook for 3 minutes on each side.
3. Add the remaining marinade after dissolving it first in the cornflour.
4. Season with extra salt and pepper and cook for 2 minutes more.
5. Serve.

Serving Suggestion: Serve with green beans.
Variation Tip: Substitute orange juice with lemon juice.
Nutritional Information per Serving:
Calories 316 | Fat 14.9g | Sodium 85mg | Carbs 11g | Fiber 0.3g | Sugar 3.8g | Protein 35.1g

Garlicky Sea Bass Fillets with Butter

Prep Time: 10 minutes
Cook Time: 8 minutes
Serves: 4
Ingredients:
- 1-pound butter
- 2 teaspoons fresh chives, minced
- 1 garlic clove, minced
- A dash of sea salt
- 4 sea bass fillets (6 ounces)
- Black pepper, to taste

- 2 tablespoons olive oil

Preparation:
1. In a mixing bowl, cream the butter until it's light and fluffy.
2. Stir in the salt, garlic, and chives until well combined.
3. Place a piece of parchment paper on top of the butter. Roll the paper into a log and place it in the refrigerator for 30 minutes.
4. Preheat your oven to 375°F.
5. Season the sea bass on both sides with black pepper and salt.
6. Melt the butter in a 9-inch cast-iron pan over medium heat.
7. Heat the oil in the pan, then add the sea bass and sear for 4 minutes on each side.
8. Remove the butter from the package, slice it, and serve it over the sea bass.
9. Serve immediately.

Serving Suggestion: Garnish with lemon slices.
Variation Tip: Substitute sea bass with cod or flounder.
Nutritional Information per Serving:
Calories 417 | Fat 37.5g | Sodium 318mg | Carbs 0.2g | Fiber 0g | Sugar 0.1g | Protein 20.3g

Seared Lobster Tails with Parsley

Prep Time: 10 minutes
Cook Time: 10 minutes
Serves: 2
Ingredients:
- 2 lobster tails, cleaned
- Sea salt and black pepper, to taste
- Pinch of red pepper flakes
- Juice of 1 lemon, divided
- 2 tablespoons olive oil
- 2 tablespoons salted butter
- 2 garlic cloves, minced
- 2 tablespoons fresh parsley leaves, minced

Preparation:
1. Season the meat side of the lobster with salt, black pepper, and red pepper flakes. Squeeze half of the lemon juice over the lobster.
2. Heat the oil and melt the butter in a cast-iron skillet over medium-high heat. Add the garlic.
3. Put the lobster in the skillet, meat-side down, and cook for 2 to 3 minutes, or until the meat is crisp and golden brown.
4. Flip the lobster, cover the skillet, and cook for 2 to 3 minutes until the lobster meat is opaque

and the shells turn red. Remove the tails from the heat.

5. Top with the remaining half of the lemon juice and the parsley and serve.

Serving Suggestion: Serve with a salad.

Variation Tip: For a milder taste, omit red pepper flakes.

Nutritional Information per Serving:

Calories 325 | Fat 26.7g | Sodium 692mg | Carbs 3.4g | Fiber 0.3g | Sugar 2.9g | Protein 0.5g

Bacon-Wrapped Scallops with Lemon Juice

Prep Time: 10 minutes
Cook Time: 20 minutes
Serves: 4
Ingredients:
- 12 large sea scallops
- 6 thin-cut bacon strips, halved lengthwise
- Pinch of sea salt
- 1 tablespoon olive oil
- 2 tablespoons salted butter, divided
- 2 garlic cloves, minced
- Juice of 1 lemon

Preparation:
1. Preheat the oven to 425°F.
2. Place a cast-iron skillet into the oven to preheat.
3. Pat the scallops dry. Wrap a halved bacon strip around each scallop, securing it with a toothpick. Season the scallops with salt.
4. Using oven mitts, remove the skillet from the oven and put the oil and one tablespoon of butter into the skillet. Stir or swirl the skillet to combine.
5. Place the wrapped scallops into the skillet and return them to the oven. Bake the scallops for 15 to 17 minutes.
6. Using oven mitts, remove the skillet from the oven, add the remaining one tablespoon of butter and the garlic and flip the scallops.
7. Let them cook in the hot skillet for 2 to 3 minutes.
8. Top with lemon juice and serve hot.

Serving Suggestion: Sprinkle minced fresh basil on top.

Variation Tip: For a spicier taste, add red pepper flakes.

Nutritional Information per Serving:

Calories 316 | Fat 23.5g | Sodium 695mg | Carbs 3.7g | Fiber 0.1g | Sugar 1.5g | Protein 21.3g

Nutty Fried Catfish

Prep Time: 10 minutes
Cook Time: 10 minutes
Serves: 6
Ingredients:
- 2 pounds' catfish fillets (3 to 4 fillets depending on size)
- 1 tablespoon Cajun seasoning
- ⅔ cup parmesan cheese
- 1 cup buttermilk
- 1 tablespoon paprika
- 1 cup ground pecans
- 2 eggs
- ⅔ cup cornmeal
- 2 cups vegetable oil

Preparation:
1. Cut the catfish into 1-inch wide strips.
2. Place the catfish strips into a large freezer bag and pour in the buttermilk. Close the bag and shake.
3. Place in the fridge, and allow the catfish to marinate for about an hour. While the catfish is marinating, whisk together the ground pecans and cornmeal.
4. Fold in the Cajun seasoning and the paprika.
5. Remove the catfish from the fridge, and remove it from the buttermilk. Discard the buttermilk.
6. Whisk the eggs together in a separate bowl.
7. Dip the catfish into the eggs so that they're completely coated. Toss them in the cornmeal mixture, and coat thoroughly.
8. Place on a baking sheet until you're ready to cook the fish.
9. In a large, 12-inch cast-iron skillet, pour in enough oil to fill the skillet about 1½ inches deep.
10. Place on the stove, and set the heat to medium-high. Bring the oil to a slow boil.
11. Place the catfish into the skillet, and fry until it's golden brown, turning as needed. This usually takes between 3 to 6 minutes.
12. You want to make sure the fish flakes with a fork. You may need to cook in batches. Remove from the oil and allow to drain.
13. Serve warm.

Serving Suggestion: Garnish with parsley.

Variation Tip: Substitute catfish with cod or haddock.

Nutritional Information per Serving:

Calories 508 | Fat 35.2g | Sodium 325mg | Carbs 13.7g | Fiber 1.4g | Sugar 2.3g | Protein 33.3g

Sautéed Spicy Shrimp

Prep Time: 10 Minutes
Cook Time: 5 Minutes
Serves: 4
Ingredients:
- 20 medium shrimp, deveined and peeled
- 1½ tablespoons olive oil
- 1 garlic clove, minced
- ½ teaspoon cumin powder
- ½ teaspoon chili powder
- ¼ teaspoon onion powder
- ¼ teaspoon salt
- 1 tablespoon olive oil
- 1 lime juice

Preparation:
1. Combine the shrimp, salt, olive oil, onion powder, chili powder, cumin, and garlic in a mixing bowl.
2. Place the seasoned shrimp in the refrigerator for 24 hours.
3. Sauté the shrimp in a 9-inch cast-iron pan with oil over medium-high heat for 5 minutes.
4. Drizzle with lime juice and serve warm.

Serving Suggestion: Garnish with parsley.
Variation Tip: For a spicier taste, add red pepper flakes.
Nutritional Information per Serving:
Calories 472 | Fat 21.5g | Sodium 1757mg | Carbs 2.2g | Fiber 0.6g | Sugar 0.1g | Protein 72.5g

Garlicky Shrimp with Fresh Cilantro

Prep Time: 10 minutes
Cook Time: 5 minutes
Serves: 4
Ingredients:
- ½ teaspoon salt
- 2 tablespoons chili garlic paste
- 3 garlic cloves, minced
- 1 tablespoon fish sauce
- 1 tablespoon soy sauce
- 1-pound large shrimp, peeled and deveined
- 1 tablespoon vegetable oil
- 2 tablespoons butter
- Juice of ½ lime
- Handful fresh cilantro, minced

Preparation:
1. Mix the salt, garlic paste, fish sauce, and soy sauce in a medium bowl.
2. Add the shrimp and stir well to coat. Heat the oil and butter over medium-high heat in a cast-iron skillet.
3. Add the shrimp and sauce, scraping every last bit from the bowl.
4. Cook for 4 to 5 minutes, frequently stirring, until the shrimp are pink all the way through.
5. Remove from the heat and transfer to a serving dish.
6. Top with the lime juice and cilantro, stir to coat and serve.

Serving Suggestion: Serve it on a bed of coconut rice.
Variation Tip: Omit chili garlic paste for a milder taste.
Nutritional Information per Serving:
Calories 184 | Fat 9.2g | Sodium 1093mg | Carbs 4.7g | Fiber 0.4g | Sugar 0.7g | Protein 22.2g

Grilled Salmon

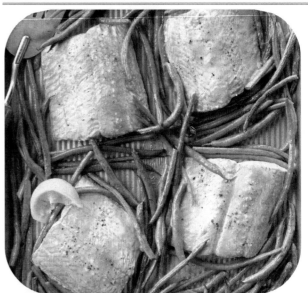

Prep Time: 10 minutes
Cook Time: 10 minutes
Serves: 4
Ingredients:
- ¾ teaspoon fresh ginger, minced
- 2 tablespoons scallions, chopped
- 1 garlic clove, minced
- ¼ cup olive oil
- 2 tablespoons low-sodium soy sauce
- ½ teaspoon dried dill weed, crushed
- 2 tablespoons balsamic vinegar
- 4 (5-ounce) boneless salmon fillets

Preparation:
1. Add all the ingredients except for the salmon to a large-sized bowl and mix well.
2. Add the salmon and coat it generously with the marinade.
3. Cover and refrigerate to marinate for at least 4–5 hours.

4. Preheat a greased cast-iron grill pan and cook the salmon fillets for about 5 minutes per side over medium heat.
5. Serve hot.
Serving Suggestions: Serve with green beans.
Variation Tip: Pat dry the salmon fillets completely before seasoning.
Nutritional Information per Serving:
Calories: 303|Fat: 21.4g|Sat Fat: 9g|Carbohydrates: 1.4g|Fiber: 0.2g|Sugar: 0.4g|Protein: 28.2g

Halibut Fillets with Vegetables

Prep Time: 10 minutes
Cook Time: 30 minutes
Serves: 2
Ingredients:
• 3 tablespoons extra-virgin olive oil
• ½ pound baby carrots
• ½ cup water, plus a little more if needed
• 3 medium leeks, sliced crosswise
• Salt and white pepper, to taste
• 3 thyme sprigs
• 1 bay leaf
• 2 skinless halibut fillets, about 1-inch thick
Preparation:
1. Preheat the oven to 375°F.
2. Heat 2 tablespoons of oil in a cast-iron skillet over medium-high heat.
3. Stir-fry the carrots until lightly golden (about 3 minutes).
4. Add the water, cover, and continue cooking until the carrots are crisp-tender (about 3 minutes).
5. Add the leeks (and a little more water, if needed), cover, and cook until soft (about 5 minutes).
6. Season with salt and pepper. Add the thyme and bay leaf.
7. Sprinkle salt and white pepper over the fish fillets and lay them on top of the vegetables.
8. Drizzle the fish with the remaining oil. Top with parchment paper and cover with a tight-fitting lid.
9. Place in the oven and bake until the fish is cooked through (about 15 minutes).
10. Discard the herbs and serve.
Serving Suggestion: Serve with rice.
Variation Tip: Replace water with fish stock.
Nutritional Information per Serving:
Calories 457 | Fat 22g | Sodium 272mg | Carbs 26g | Fiber 6.6g | Sugar 10.7g | Protein 42g

Pan-Fried Crab Cakes

Prep Time: 10 minutes
Cook Time: 10 minutes
Serves: 4
Ingredients:
• 1-pound lump blue crabmeat
• ½ cup breadcrumbs
• 1 egg, lightly beaten
• Juice of 1 lemon, divided
• Zest of 1 lemon
• 1 tablespoon fresh oregano leaves, minced
• 1 tablespoon fresh thyme leaves, minced
• 1 tablespoon fresh chives, minced
• Pinch of sea salt and black pepper
• 4 tablespoons salted butter
Preparation:
1. Mix the crabmeat, breadcrumbs, egg, half of the lemon juice, lemon zest, oregano, thyme, chives, sea salt, and black pepper in a large bowl. Form the mixture into four crab cakes.
2. In a cast-iron skillet over medium-high heat, melt the butter.
3. Sear the crab cakes for 4 minutes per side.
4. Top with the remaining lemon juice, and serve.
Serving Suggestion: Serve on a bed of zucchini noodles.
Variation Tip: Add one minced jalapeño pepper in place of the thyme and oregano for a spicy alternative.
Nutritional Information per Serving:
Calories 226 | Fat 13.6g | Sodium 514mg | Carbs 12.5g | Fiber 1.7g | Sugar 2.6g | Protein 13.6g

Blackened Sea Bass with Lemon Juice

Prep Time: 10 minutes
Cook Time: 10 minutes
Serves: 4
Ingredients:
• 1 teaspoon dried oregano
• 1 teaspoon freshly ground black pepper

- 1 teaspoon sea salt
- ½ teaspoon cayenne
- ¼ teaspoon red pepper flakes
- ¼ teaspoon ground cumin
- 1 teaspoon smoked paprika
- 4 (4-ounce) sea bass fillets, cleaned and patted dry
- 4 tablespoons salted butter, melted
- Juice of 1 lemon

Preparation:
1. Stir together the oregano, pepper, salt, cayenne, red pepper flakes, cumin, and paprika in a small bowl. Set aside.
2. Heat a dry cast-iron skillet over medium-high heat.
3. Brush each fish fillet on both sides with the melted butter and carefully coat both sides with the spice mixture.
4. Add the fillets to the hot skillet and cook for 2 to 3 minutes per side until blackened and cooked through.
5. Drizzle the lemon juice over the fish and serve.

Serving Suggestion: Garnish with parsley.
Variation Tip: For a spicier result, substitute chipotle powder for the smoked paprika.
Nutritional Information per Serving:
Calories 153 | Fat 3.3g | Sodium 568mg | Carbs 2.7g | Fiber 0.9g | Sugar 1.6g | Protein 27.2g

Maple-Glazed Salmon Fillets

Prep Time: 10 minutes
Cook Time: 20 minutes
Serves: 2
Ingredients:
- 2 tablespoons soy sauce
- 1 tablespoon maple syrup
- 2 garlic cloves, minced
- 1 tablespoon fresh ginger, peeled and minced
- Juice of 1 lime
- ¼ teaspoon paprika
- 1 tablespoon olive oil
- 2 (4-ounce) salmon fillets

Preparation:
1. Whisk the soy sauce, maple syrup, garlic, ginger, lime juice, and paprika to combine in a small bowl.
2. Preheat the oven to 375°F.
3. Spread the oil evenly over the bottom of a cast-iron skillet. Place the salmon into the skillet, skin-side down.
4. Reserve 2 tablespoons of the sauce, then spoon what remains over the salmon.

5. Bake for 15 minutes, or until the salmon begins to brown and the flesh is opaque.
6. Using oven mitts, remove the salmon from the oven. Set the broiler to high.
7. Spoon the reserved sauce over the salmon.
8. Return the salmon to the oven and broil for 2 to 3 minutes, or until a golden crust forms on the salmon.
9. Remove from the oven and serve.

Serving Suggestion: Serve with greens
Variation Tip: Substitute maple syrup with honey.
Nutritional Information per Serving:
Calories 257 | Fat 14.1g | Sodium 954mg | Carbs 11.4g | Fiber 0.4g | Sugar 7g | Protein 23.3g

Honey Mustard Salmon Fillets

Prep Time: 10 minutes
Cook Time: 8 minutes
Serves: 4
Ingredients:
- 1 tablespoon honey
- 1 (1-inch) piece fresh ginger, grated finely
- 1 tablespoon lemon juice, freshly squeezed
- 2 tablespoons olive oil
- 2 tablespoons fresh parsley, chopped
- 1 tablespoon Dijon mustard
- 4 (6-ounce) salmon fillets

Preparation:
1. Mix the honey, ginger, lemon juice, and mustard in a bowl. Set aside.
2. Heat the olive oil in a large-sized cast-iron wok and cook the salmon fillets for about 4 minutes per side over medium-high heat.
3. Stir in the honey mixture and immediately remove from the heat.
4. Serve hot.

Serving Suggestion: Serve with fresh green beans.
Variation Tip: You can also use lime juice.
Nutritional Information per Serving:
Calories: 305|Fat: 17.7g| Sat Fat: 7.1g|Carbohydrates: 4.7g|Fiber: 0.2g|Sugar: 4.4g|Protein: 33.3g

Creamy Zucchini Noodles with Parmesan Cheese

Prep Time: 15 minutes
Cook Time: 10 minutes
Serves: 4
Ingredients:
• ¼ cup mayonnaise
• 1¼ cups heavy whipping cream
• Salt and black pepper, to taste
• 4 egg yolks
• 2 tablespoons fresh parsley, chopped
• 30 ounces' zucchini, spiralized
• 3 ounces' parmesan cheese, grated
• 2 tablespoons butter, melted
Preparation:
1. In a cast-iron saucepan, add the heavy cream and let it reach a gentle boil.
2. Switch the heat to low and cook until reduced.
3. Add the mayonnaise, salt, and black pepper and cook until the mixture is warmed through.
4. Add the zucchini noodles and gently stir to combine.
5. Immediately remove from the heat.
6. Divide the mixture evenly between four serving plates.
7. Top with the egg yolks, followed by the parmesan and parsley.
8. Drizzle with butter and serve.
Serving Suggestion: Serve alongside chicken wings.
Variation Tip: You can also use some cheddar cheese for this recipe.
Nutritional Information per Serving:
Calories: 427|Fat: 39.1g|Sat Fat: 7.9g|Carbohydrates: 9.7|Fiber: 2.4g|Sugar: 3.8g|Protein: 13g

Summer Squash Gratin with Cheese

Prep Time: 15 minutes
Cook Time: 35 minutes
Serves: 4
Ingredients:
• ¾ cup panko breadcrumbs
• 4 tablespoons olive oil, divided
• ½ cup parmesan cheese, grated
• 2 garlic cloves, minced
• 1 tablespoon fresh thyme leaves
• Salt and black pepper, as required
• 2 medium shallots, sliced thinly
• 2 pounds' summer squash, cut into ¼-inch pieces crosswise
• 1 teaspoon lemon zest, grated finely
Preparation:
1. Preheat the oven to 400°F. Arrange a rack in the middle of the oven.
2. In a bowl, add half the olive oil, breadcrumbs, and parmesan cheese and mix until well combined.
3. In an 8-inch cast-iron wok, heat the remaining oil over medium heat and cook the shallots for about 3–4 minutes, stirring occasionally.
4. Add the garlic and cook for about 1 minute.
5. Remove from the heat and stir in the squash, thyme, lemon zest, salt, and black pepper.
6. Spread the squash mixture into an even layer and sprinkle with the breadcrumb mixture evenly.
7. Bake for about 30 minutes.
8. Remove from the oven and set aside for about 5 minutes before serving.
Serving Suggestion: Serve topped with more shredded cheese.
Variation Tip: You can also add some mozzarella.
Nutritional Information per Serving:
Calories: 283|Fat: 18.5g|Sat Fat: 6.7g|Carbohydrates: 14.4g|Fiber: 2.7g|Sugar: 8.1g|Protein: 7.2g

Roasted Cauliflower Florets

Prep Time: 10 minutes
Cook Time: 35 minutes
Serves: 4
Ingredients:
- 1 medium cauliflower, cut into florets
- ½ teaspoon ground coriander
- 1 tablespoon canola oil
- ½ teaspoon smoked paprika
- Pepper
- Salt

Preparation:
1. Preheat the oven to 400°F.
2. In a bowl, toss the cauliflower florets with the oil, coriander, paprika, pepper, and salt until well coated.
3. Add the cauliflower florets to a cast-iron skillet and roast in the preheated oven for 35 minutes.

Serving Suggestion: Garnish with fresh cilantro and serve.
Variation Tip: Add your choice of seasonings.
Nutritional Information Per Serving:
Calories 68 | Fat 3g | Sodium 82mg | Carbs 7g | Fiber 3.7g | Sugar 3.5g | Protein 2.9g

Delectable Veggie Fajitas

Prep Time: 10 minutes
Cook Time: 10 minutes
Serves: 4
Ingredients:
- 1 medium onion, sliced
- 1 green bell pepper, sliced
- 1 red bell pepper, sliced
- 1 teaspoon chili powder
- ½ teaspoon paprika
- 2 tablespoons canola oil
- 1 teaspoon curry powder
- Pepper
- Salt

Preparation:

1. In a mixing bowl, mix the bell peppers, onion, chili powder, paprika, curry powder, pepper, and salt until well combined.
2. Heat the oil in a cast-iron skillet over medium heat.
3. Add the veggie mixture to the skillet and sauté for 8–10 minutes or until the veggies are tender.

Serving Suggestion: Serve in tortillas with your favorite toppings.
Variation Tip: You can also add your choice of seasonings.
Nutritional Information Per Serving:
Calories 96 | Fat 7g | Sodium 48mg | Carbs 7g | Fiber 2g | Sugar 4g | Protein 1g

Scrambled Rice with Pineapple and Onion

Prep Time: 10 minutes
Cook Time: 10 minutes
Serves: 4
Ingredients:
- 3 cups cooked brown rice
- 2 cups pineapple, diced
- ½ cup frozen peas
- 2 garlic cloves, minced
- 2 tablespoons olive oil
- ½ teaspoon ginger powder
- 1 tablespoon sesame oil
- 3 tablespoons soy sauce
- ¼ cup green onion, sliced
- ½ cup frozen corn
- 2 carrots, peeled and grated
- 1 onion, diced

Preparation:
1. Whisk the soy sauce, ginger powder, and sesame oil in a small bowl and set aside.
2. Heat the oil in a cast-iron pan over medium-high heat.
3. Add the onion and garlic and sauté for 3–4 minutes.
4. Add the carrots, corn, and peas and stir constantly for 3–4 minutes.
5. Add the rice, pineapple, green onions, and soy sauce mixture and stir for 2–3 minutes.

Serving Suggestion: Garnish with parsley and serve.
Variation Tip: You can also add ¼ cup of cashews.
Nutritional Information Per Serving:
Calories 714 | Fat 14g | Sodium 724mg | Carbs 133g | Fiber 9g | Sugar 12g | Protein 14g

Stir-Fried Spicy Cabbage

Prep Time: 10 minutes
Cook Time: 10 minutes
Serves: 4
Ingredients:
• 1 cabbage head, sliced
• 2 green onions, sliced
• 1 tablespoon ginger, minced
• 2 tablespoons canola oil
• 2 garlic cloves, minced
• 1 tablespoon soy sauce
• ½ tablespoon vinegar
• 4 dried chilies
• ½ teaspoon salt
Preparation:
1. Heat the oil in a cast-iron skillet over medium heat.
2. Add the ginger, green onion, and garlic and sauté for 2–3 minutes.
3. Add the dried chilies and sauté for 30 seconds.
4. Add the cabbage, soy sauce, vinegar, and salt and stir fry for 1–2 minutes over high heat or until the cabbage is wilted.
Serving Suggestion: Garnish with parsley and serve.
Variation Tip: You can also add liquid aminos instead of soy sauce.
Nutritional Information Per Serving:
Calories 118 | Fat 7g | Sodium 550mg | Carbs 12g | Fiber 4.9g | Sugar 6g | Protein 2.9g

Sautéed Carrots and Snow Peas

Prep Time: 10 minutes
Cook Time: 10 minutes
Serves: 4
Ingredients:
• 2 medium zucchini, cut into matchsticks
• 2 cups carrots, cut into matchsticks
• 2 tablespoons canola oil
• 2 teaspoons garlic, minced
• 2 cups snow peas
• 1 teaspoon sesame seeds
• 1 tablespoon honey
• 3 tablespoons soy sauce
Preparation:
1. Mix the soy sauce, honey, and garlic in a small bowl and set aside.
2. Heat the oil in a cast-iron skillet over medium-high heat.
3. Add the carrots, zucchini, and snow peas and sauté for 1–2 minutes.
4. Add the soy sauce mixture and stir fry for 1 minute.
Serving Suggestion: Garnish with sesame seeds and serve.
Variation Tip: You can add your choice of seasonings.
Nutritional Information Per Serving:
Calories 162 | Fat 7g | Sodium 728mg | Carbs 20g | Fiber 4g | Sugar 12g | Protein 5.3g

Healthy Zucchini Noodles with Sesame Seeds

Prep Time: 10 minutes
Cook Time: 10 minutes
Serves: 4
Ingredients:
• 4 small zucchinis, spiralized
• 2 onions, spiralized
• 2 tablespoons canola oil
• 1 tablespoon sesame seeds
• 2 tablespoons teriyaki sauce
• 1 tablespoon soy sauce
• Pepper
• Salt
Preparation:
1. Heat the oil in a cast-iron skillet over medium heat.
2. Add the onion and sauté for 5 minutes.
3. Add the zucchini noodles and cook for 2 minutes.
4. Add the teriyaki sauce, sesame seeds, and soy sauce and cook for 5 minutes.
Serving Suggestion: Garnish with parsley and serve.
Variation Tip: Add ¼ teaspoon of crushed red pepper flakes.
Nutritional Information Per Serving:
Calories 126 | Fat 8g | Sodium 623mg | Carbs 11g | Fiber 2.8g | Sugar 5.7g | Protein 3.2g

Parmesan Risotto in Vegetable Broth

Prep Time: 10 minutes
Cook Time: 50 minutes
Serves: 6
Ingredients:
- 1½ cups Arborio rice
- 2 tablespoons green onion, sliced
- ¾ cup frozen green peas
- ¼ teaspoon black pepper
- 2½ tablespoons butter
- ½ cup dry white wine
- 1 cup parmesan cheese, grated
- 5 cups vegetable broth
- 1½ teaspoons kosher salt

Preparation:
1. Preheat the oven to 350°F.
2. Add 4 cups of broth and the rice to a cast-iron Dutch oven.
3. Cover and bake in the preheated oven for 45 minutes.
4. Remove from the oven. Add the remaining broth, parmesan cheese, butter, dry white wine, pepper, and salt and stir for 2–3 minutes.
5. Add the green peas and stir for 2 minutes.

Serving Suggestion: Garnish with green onion and serve.
Variation Tip: You can also add vegetable stock instead of broth.
Nutritional Information Per Serving:
Calories 325 | Fat 9g | Sodium 1372mg | Carbs 41g | Fiber 2g | Sugar 1.8g | Protein 13g

Healthy Couscous with Almonds

Prep Time: 10 minutes
Cook Time: 5 minutes
Serves: 8
Ingredients:

- 2 cups couscous
- 6 tablespoons almonds, sliced
- 2 garlic cloves, minced
- 2 tablespoons canola oil
- 2¼ cups water
- ½ cup fresh parsley, chopped
- 1 teaspoon paprika
- ¾ teaspoon kosher salt

Preparation:
1. Heat the oil in a cast-iron Dutch oven over medium-high heat.
2. Add the garlic and almonds and sauté for 2 minutes.
3. Add the paprika and stir for 20 seconds.
4. Add the water and stir well. Bring to a boil.
5. Remove the Dutch oven from the heat.
6. Add the couscous and salt and stir well. Cover and let the mixture sit until all the liquid is absorbed.
7. Fluff the couscous with a fork.

Serving Suggestion: Garnish with parsley and serve.
Variation Tip: You can also add vegetable stock instead of water.
Nutritional Information Per Serving:
Calories 223 | Fat 6g | Sodium 226mg | Carbs 35g | Fiber 3g | Sugar 0.3g | Protein 6g

Parmesan Asparagus

Prep Time: 10 minutes
Cook Time: 10 minutes
Serves: 3
Ingredients:
- 2 tablespoons salted butter
- 2 pounds' asparagus, woody ends trimmed
- Juice of 1 lemon
- Pinch of sea salt
- ¼ cup parmesan cheese, grated

Preparation:
1. Melt the butter in a cast-iron skillet over medium heat.
2. Put the asparagus in the pan and toss to coat with the butter. Cover with a lid. Cook for 3 to 4 minutes, then turn the asparagus.
3. Re-cover and cook for an additional 3 to 4 minutes until the asparagus is bright green.
4. Transfer to a plate and top with lemon juice, salt, and parmesan.
5. Serve warm.

Serving Suggestion: Serve with roast meat.
Variation Tip: Replace butter with olive oil.
Nutritional Information per Serving:
Calories 238 | Fat 15.1g | Sodium 442mg | Carbs 14.3g | Fiber 6.4g | Sugar 7.6g | Protein 17.3g

Roasted Baby Potatoes

Prep Time: 10 minutes
Cook Time: 50 minutes
Serves: 6
Ingredients:
- 1½ pounds baby potatoes
- 2 thyme sprigs
- ½ teaspoon paprika
- 3 tablespoons canola oil
- 3 garlic cloves, crushed
- Pepper
- Salt

Preparation:
1. Preheat the oven to 450°F.
2. Add the potatoes to a large pot and cover with water. Season with salt and bring to a boil.
3. Cook the potatoes until tender. Drain well and transfer to a cast-iron skillet.
4. Gently smash each potato. Add the thyme, paprika, and garlic over the potatoes.
5. Drizzle with the oil and season with salt and pepper.
6. Roast the potatoes in the oven for 35–40 minutes.

Serving Suggestion: Garnish with parsley and serve.

Variation Tip: Once the potatoes are baked, sprinkle them with 2 tablespoons of grated parmesan cheese.

Nutritional Information Per Serving:
Calories 130 | Fat 7g | Sodium 39mg | Carbs 14g | Fiber 3g | Sugar 0g | Protein 3g

Wok-Cooked Broccoli and Cauliflower

Prep Time: 15 minutes
Cook Time: 8 minutes
Serves: 6
Ingredients:

- 4 cups fresh broccoli florets
- 3 shallots, chopped
- ½ cup vegetable broth
- 2 cups fresh cauliflower florets
- 1 teaspoon dried basil, crushed
- Ground black pepper, to taste
- ½ teaspoon seasoned salt

Preparation:
1. In a large cast-iron wok, combine all the ingredients and mix well.
2. Place the wok over medium heat and cook for about 8 minutes, stirring occasionally.
3. Serve hot.

Serving Suggestions: Serve with roast chicken.

Variation Tip: You can also add potatoes to this recipe.

Nutritional Information per Serving:
Calories: 38|Fat: 0.4g|Sat Fat: 0g|Carbohydrates: 7.3g|Fiber: 2.4g|Sugar: 1.9g|Protein: 3g

Sautéed Cabbage and Apple

Prep Time: 15 minutes
Cook Time: 15 minutes
Serves: 5
Ingredients:
- 1 large apple, cored and sliced thinly
- 1½ pounds cabbage, chopped finely
- 1 Serrano pepper, chopped
- 2 teaspoons coconut oil
- 1 onion, sliced thinly
- 1 tablespoon fresh thyme, chopped
- 1 tablespoon apple cider vinegar
- ⅔ cup almonds, chopped

Preparation:
1. In a cast-iron wok, melt 1 teaspoon of coconut oil and stir fry the apple for about 3 minutes over medium heat.
2. Move the apple to a bowl.
3. In the same wok, melt 1 teaspoon of coconut oil over medium heat and sauté the onion for about 2 minutes.
4. Add the cabbage and sauté for about 7 minutes.
5. Add the apple, thyme, and vinegar and cook, covered, for about 2 minutes.
6. Serve warm garnished with almonds.

Serving Suggestion: Serve with baked potatoes.

Variation Tip: You can use both purple and green cabbage.

Nutritional Information per Serving:
Calories: 157|Fat: 8.4g|Sat Fat: 0.3g|Carbohydrates: 19.3g|Fiber: 6.8g|Sugar: 10.5g|Protein: 4.9g

Wok-Fried Mushroom with Spinach and Scallion

Prep Time: 15 minutes
Cook Time: 12 minutes
Serves: 2
Ingredients:
- ½ tablespoon fresh ginger, grated
- 1 tablespoon olive oil
- 2 cups fresh mushrooms, sliced
- ½ bunch fresh spinach, chopped
- 1 tablespoon soy sauce
- Salt and black pepper, to taste
- 2 scallions, chopped

Preparation:
1. In a cast-iron wok, heat the oil and sauté the ginger for about 1 minute over medium-high heat.
2. Add the mushrooms and salt and sauté for about 6 minutes.
3. Add the spinach and cook for about 3 minutes.
4. Stir in the scallion, soy sauce, and black pepper and cook for about 2 minutes.
5. Serve hot.

Serving Suggestion: Serve alongside your favorite rice.
Variation Tip: You can use mushrooms of your choice.
Nutritional Information per Serving:
Calories: 109|Fat: 7.7g|Sat Fat: 0.3g|Carbohydrates: 8.2g|Fiber: 3.3g|Sugar: 2.1g|Protein: 5.6g

Lemony Quinoa and Asparagus

Prep Time: 15 minutes
Cook Time: 18 minutes
Serves: 4
Ingredients:
- 2 teaspoons coconut oil
- 1-pound fresh asparagus, trimmed
- ½ onion, chopped
- 1 cup red quinoa, cooked
- ½ cup parmesan cheese, shredded
- 2 garlic cloves, minced
- 1 tablespoon ground turmeric
- 1 tablespoon freshly squeezed lemon juice

Preparation:
1. In a pot full of boiling water, cook the asparagus for about 3 minutes.
2. Drain well and rinse under cold water.
3. In a large-sized cast-iron wok, melt the coconut oil and sauté the onion and garlic for about 5 minutes over medium heat.
4. Stir in the quinoa, turmeric, and broth and cook for about 6 minutes.
5. Stir in the parmesan, lemon juice, and asparagus and cook for about 4 minutes.

Serving Suggestion: Serve topped with mushrooms.
Variation Tip: You can also use barley in this recipe.
Nutritional Information per Serving:
Calories: 255|Fat: 7.9g|Sat Fat: 0.8g|Carbohydrates: 35g|Fiber: 6.1g|Sugar: 2.9g|Protein: 12.7g

Carrots and Snow Peas with Shallot

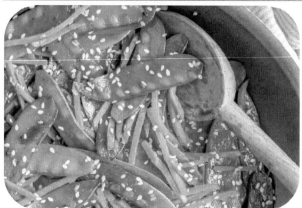

Prep Time: 15 minutes
Cook Time: 6 minutes
Serves: 4
Ingredients:
- 1¾ cups fresh carrots, peeled and sliced
- 2 tablespoons butter
- 2¾ cups fresh snow peas
- Salt, to taste
- 1 shallot, minced
- 1 tablespoon vegetable broth

Preparation:
1. Heat the butter in a large cast-iron wok and stir fry the carrots for about 3 minutes over medium heat.
2. Add the snow peas, shallots, and salt and stir fry for about 2 minutes.
3. Stir in the broth and stir fry for about 1 minute.
4. Remove from the heat and serve hot.

Serving Suggestion: Serve topped with sesame seeds.
Variation Tip: It's best to use fresh carrots and snow peas.
Nutritional Information per Serving:
Calories: 121|Fat: 6g|Sat Fat: 0.3g|Carbohydrates: 13.3g|Fiber: 4.3g|Sugar: 6.8g|Protein: 4.2g

Brussels Sprouts Casserole with Cheeses

Prep Time: 10 minutes
Cook Time: 40 minutes
Serves: 6
Ingredients:
- 2 pounds Brussels sprouts, cut in half
- 1 cup parmesan cheese, grated
- 1¼ cups milk
- 1½ tablespoons flour
- ½ teaspoon garlic powder
- ¼ cup mayonnaise
- 2½ tablespoons butter
- ½ teaspoon salt

Preparation:
1. Preheat the oven to 375°F.
2. Melt the butter in a cast-iron skillet over medium heat.
3. Add the flour and stir continuously to remove any clumps.
4. Turn off the heat. Add the milk, cheese, garlic powder, mayonnaise, and salt and stir until the cheese is melted.
5. Add the Brussels sprouts and stir well to combine.
6. Bake in the preheated oven for 40 minutes.

Serving Suggestion: Garnish with parsley and serve.
Variation Tip: Add your choice of seasonings.
Nutritional Information Per Serving:
Calories 227 | Fat 12g | Sodium 474mg | Carbs 20g | Fiber 5g | Sugar 6g | Protein 12g

Zucchini and Ripe Tomato Gratin

Prep Time: 10 minutes
Cook Time: 25 minutes
Serves: 4
Ingredients:
- 2 large ripe tomatoes, cut into ¼-inch slices
- 1 large zucchini, cut into ¼-inch slices
- ¼ cup olive oil
- 3 garlic cloves, minced
- 1 cup parmesan cheese, grated
- ½ teaspoon sea salt
- 1 tablespoon fresh oregano, minced
- 1 tablespoon fresh thyme, minced

Preparation:
1. Heat the oven to 375°F.
2. In a cast-iron skillet, arrange the tomatoes and the zucchini in alternating rows, overlapping a little so they stand up.
3. Drizzle with the olive oil and top with the garlic.
4. Mix the parmesan, salt, oregano, and thyme in a small bowl. Sprinkle the mixture over the top of the vegetables.
5. Bake for 20 to 25 minutes, until the zucchini is cooked through and the cheese has formed a golden crust.
6. Serve warm.

Serving Suggestion: Serve with grilled meats.
Variation Tip: To make this a heartier dish, add thinly sliced red potatoes.
Nutritional Information per Serving:
Calories 348 | Fat 26.6g | Sodium 832mg | Carbs 10.4g | Fiber 2.8g | Sugar 3.9g | Protein 22.4g

Honey Sriracha Brussels Sprouts

Prep Time: 10 minutes
Cook Time: 30 minutes
Serves: 4
Ingredients:
- 2 tablespoons honey
- 1 tablespoon sriracha
- ¼ cup soy sauce
- 20 Brussels sprouts, stemmed and halved

Preparation:
1. Preheat the oven to 400°F.
2. Whisk the honey, sriracha, and soy sauce to blend in a small bowl.
3. In a cast-iron skillet, combine the Brussels sprouts and sauce and toss well to coat.
4. Roast for 20 minutes in the oven, stir well and return to the oven. Turn the broiler to high and broil for 5 to 7 minutes, or until crispy.
5. Serve.

Serving Suggestion: Serve with pork chops.
Variation Tip: Substitute sriracha with red chili paste.
Nutritional Information per Serving:
Calories 85 | Fat 0.3g | Sodium 949mg | Carbs 19.3g | Fiber 3.7g | Sugar 10.9g | Protein 4.3g

Garlicky Green Beans

Prep Time: 10 minutes
Cook Time: 10 minutes
Serves: 4
Ingredients:
• 3 tablespoons salted butter
• 1-pound fresh green beans, ends removed
• 2 garlic cloves, minced
• Pinch of sea salt
Preparation:
1. In a cast-iron skillet over medium heat, melt the butter.
2. Add the green beans and cook for 3 to 5 minutes, stirring occasionally.
3. Add the garlic and the salt, stir well, cover the skillet, and cook for 5 minutes.
4. Serve.
Serving Suggestion: Serve with roast chicken.
Variation Tip: Reduce the cooking time to 2 minutes after adding the garlic for al dente green beans.
Nutritional Information per Serving:
Calories 114 | Fat 8.8g | Sodium 127mg | Carbs 8.6g | Fiber 3.9g | Sugar 1.6g | Protein 2.3g

Roasted Vegetable Mixture

Prep Time: 10 minutes
Cook Time: 40 minutes
Serves: 4
Ingredients:
• 1 large purple beet, peeled and cubed
• 1 large golden beet, peeled and cubed
• 1 sweet potato, peeled and cubed
• 5 small red potatoes, quartered
• 1 parsnip, peeled and cubed
• 5 carrots, peeled and sliced
• 1 yellow onion, diced
• ¼ cup olive oil
• 1 tablespoon herbes de Provence
• 3 garlic cloves, minced
• 1 teaspoon sea salt
Preparation:
1. Heat the oven to 400°F.

2. Combine the beets, potatoes, parsnip, carrots, and onion with olive oil, herbes de Provence, garlic, and salt in a cast-iron skillet.
3. Mix well to coat and spread the vegetables evenly over the bottom of the skillet.
4. Roast in the oven for 25 minutes, stir well, and roast for an additional 15 to 20 minutes.
5. When the vegetables are cooked through and browning around the edges, remove them from the heat.
6. Stir well to distribute the juices before serving.
Serving Suggestion: Garnish with parsley.
Variation Tip: Root vegetables are a lovely base for herbs and spices. Fresh herbs, curry, turmeric, and a dash of cayenne are a great addition, too.
Nutritional Information per Serving:
Calories 412 | Fat 15.7g | Sodium 622mg | Carbs 63.1g | Fiber 11.1g | Sugar 15.9g | Protein 9.1g

Baked Yukon Gold Potatoes

Prep Time: 10 minutes
Cook Time: 1 hour
Serves: 5
Ingredients:
• 5 Yukon gold potatoes
• 8 tablespoons (1 stick) salted butter, cubed
• 4 garlic cloves, minced
• 1½ teaspoons sea salt
• ½ teaspoon red pepper flakes
• Olive oil, for brushing
• ¼ cup parmesan cheese, grated
• 2 tablespoons fresh parsley leaves, minced
Preparation:
1. Preheat the oven to 425°F.
2. Without cutting through the bottom skin, cut the potatoes crosswise into ½-inch slices.
3. Arrange the potatoes in a cast-iron skillet and sprinkle them with the butter, followed by the garlic, salt, red pepper flakes, and roast for 30 minutes.
4. Brush the potatoes with oil and bake for 30 minutes more.
5. Sprinkle the potatoes with parmesan cheese and fresh parsley.
Serving Suggestion: Serve with chicken or fish.
Variation Tip: Omit red pepper flakes for a milder taste.
Nutritional Information per Serving:
Calories 374 | Fat 25.1g | Sodium 2365mg | Carbs 32g | Fiber 2.5g | Sugar 1.2g | Protein 9.3g

Roasted Cabbage Strips

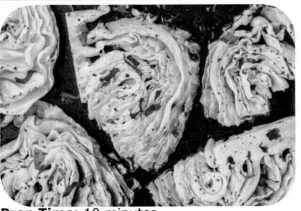

Prep Time: 10 minutes
Cook Time: 20 minutes
Serves: 4
Ingredients:
- 1 small head white cabbage
- 1 tablespoon olive oil
- Pinch of sea salt
- Pinch of red pepper flakes
- 2 tablespoons apple cider vinegar (optional)

Preparation:
1. Heat the oven to 400°F.
2. Halve the cabbage and then slice each half into ½-inch thick strips.
3. Toss the cabbage with olive oil, salt, and red pepper flakes in your cast-iron skillet.
4. Spread the cabbage evenly across the bottom of the skillet.
5. Roast in the oven for 15 minutes, stir and then roast for an additional 3 to 5 minutes.
6. Finish with the apple cider vinegar (if using) to serve.

Serving Suggestion: Serve with chicken thighs or a citrusy vinaigrette.
Variation Tip: Omit red pepper flakes for a milder taste.
Nutritional Information per Serving:
Calories 76 | Fat 3.7g | Sodium 91mg | Carbs 10.5g | Fiber 4.5g | Sugar 5.8g | Protein 2.3g

Light Fried Broccoli

Prep Time: 10 minutes
Cook Time: 10 minutes
Serves: 4
Ingredients:
- 4 tablespoons sesame oil, divided
- 1 head broccoli, separated into florets and halved
- 1 tablespoon soy sauce
- 3 garlic cloves, minced

Preparation:

1. Heat two tablespoons of sesame oil in a cast-iron skillet over medium-high heat.
2. Put the broccoli in the hot skillet, evenly distributing it across the bottom.
3. Cook for 2 to 3 minutes without turning.
4. Flip the broccoli and add the soy sauce, remaining sesame oil, and garlic. Cover the skillet and cook for another 2 to 3 minutes.
5. Serve warm.

Serving Suggestion: Garnish with sesame seeds.
Variation Tip: You can also use broccoli, particularly because the stalks also get a nice char.
Nutritional Information per Serving:
Calories 141 | Fat 13.8g | Sodium 241mg | Carbs 4.1g | Fiber 1.3g | Sugar 0.9g | Protein 1.7g

Cauliflower Steaks with Butter Mixture

Prep Time: 10 minutes
Cook Time: 20 minutes
Serves: 2
Ingredients:
- ¼ cup olive oil
- 1 head cauliflower, cut into ½-inch thick slices
- ½ teaspoon sea salt
- ¼ teaspoon freshly ground black pepper
- 4 tablespoons butter, melted
- 1 cup fresh parsley, coarsely chopped
- 2 garlic cloves, minced
- Juice of 1 lemon

Preparation:
1. Heat the oven to 375°F.
2. Heat the olive oil in a cast-iron skillet over medium-high heat.
3. When the oil is hot, arrange the cauliflower steaks in the skillet and sprinkle with salt and pepper.
4. Cook for 2 to 3 minutes, then flip and cook for another 2 to 3 minutes.
5. Transfer the skillet to the oven and bake for 10 to 12 minutes, until the cauliflower is cooked through and browned.
6. While the cauliflower is cooking, mix the butter, parsley, and garlic in a small bowl.
7. When the cauliflower comes out of the oven, brush each steak with the butter mixture and top with a squeeze of lemon juice before serving.

Serving Suggestion: Serve with a zesty salad.
Variation Tip: Add smoked paprika for more flavor.
Nutritional Information per Serving:
Calories 475 | Fat 48.7g | Sodium 689mg | Carbs 12.2g | Fiber 4.5g | Sugar 6.4g | Protein 4.1g

Baked Marinated Beans

Prep Time: 15 minutes
Cook Time: 50 minutes
Serves: 4
Ingredients:
• ½ cup green bell pepper, chopped
• 3 garlic cloves, minced
• 1¼ cups tomato sauce
• ¼ cup water
• 1 tablespoon olive oil
• ½ cup white onion, chopped
• Salt, as required
• 5 tablespoons pure maple syrup
• 1 tablespoon liquid smoke
• Ground black pepper, to taste
• ¼ cup Worcestershire sauce
• 2 (14-ounce) cans great northern beans, rinsed and drained
Preparation:
1. Preheat the oven to 325ºF.
2. Heat the oil in a large cast-iron wok and cook the bell pepper, onion, garlic, and salt for about 5 minutes over medium heat.
3. Add the remaining ingredients except for the beans and stir to combine.
4. Add the beans and gently stir to combine.
5. Put the wok into the oven and bake for about 45 minutes.
6. Serve hot.
Serving Suggestions: Serve alongside sausages and toast.
Variation Tip: You can also use red bell peppers.
Nutritional Information per Serving:
Calories: 394|Fat: 3.9g|Sat Fat: 0.4g|Carbohydrates: 75.6g|Fiber: 16.2g|Sugar: 22g|Protein: 16.3g

Spicy Quinoa

Prep Time: 10 minutes
Cook Time: 25 minutes
Serves: 4
Ingredients:
• 1 teaspoon curry powder
• 2 tablespoons olive oil
• 1 teaspoon ground turmeric
• 1 cup quinoa, uncooked, rinsed, and drained
• ¾ cup almonds, toasted
• ¾ cup fresh parsley, chopped
• ½ teaspoon ground cumin
• 2 cups vegetable broth
• ½ cup raisins
Preparation:
1. In a medium-sized cast-iron saucepan, heat the oil and sauté the curry powder, turmeric, and cumin for about 2 minutes over medium-low heat.
2. Add the quinoa and sauté for about 3 minutes.
3. Add the broth and stir to combine.
4. Switch the heat to low and simmer, covered, for about 20 minutes.
5. Remove the saucepan from the heat and set aside, covered, for about 5 minutes.
6. In the pan of the quinoa mixture, add the almonds and raisins and toss to coat.
7. Drizzle with lemon juice and serve.
Serving Suggestion: Serve alongside roasted veggies.
Variation Tip: You can use your favorite nuts.
Nutritional Information per Serving:
Calories: 402|Fat: 19.5g|Sat Fat: 5.8g|Carbohydrates: 47.4g|Fiber: 6.6g|Sugar: 12g|Protein: 13.2g

Pan-Fried Creamy Cauliflower and Cheese

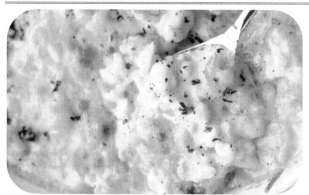

Prep Time: 15 minutes
Cook Time: 15 minutes
Serves: 4
Ingredients:
• 1 large head cauliflower, cut into florets
• 1 cup water
• ½ teaspoon salt
• 1 tablespoon olive oil
• 1 cup heavy cream
• 1 teaspoon garlic powder
• ½ teaspoon yellow mustard
• Ground black pepper, to taste
• 12 ounces' cheddar cheese, grated
Preparation:
1. In a cast-iron wok, heat the oil and stir in the cauliflower over medium-high heat.

2. Stir in the cream, water, garlic powder, salt, and mustard, and let it reach a gentle boil.
3. Cook for about 10 minutes with the lid on until thick, stirring often.
4. Meanwhile, preheat your oven's broiler.
5. In the wok, add 8 ounces of cheese and stir to combine.
6. Remove from the heat and sprinkle with the remaining cheese and black pepper.
7. Move the wok to the oven and broil for about 3 minutes.
8. Serve hot.
Serving Suggestion: Serve alongside roasted veggies.
Variation Tip: You can also add some mozzarella cheese to add stringiness.
Nutritional Information per Serving:
Calories: 496|Fat: 42.9g|Sat Fat: 8.6g|Carbohydrates: 6g|Fiber: 1.8g|Sugar: 2.2g|Protein: 23.3g

Fried Flour-Coated Okra

Prep Time: 10 minutes
Cook Time: 15 minutes
Serves: 5
Ingredients:
• 2 cups all-purpose flour, divided
• 1 teaspoon sea salt, divided
• 1 teaspoon cayenne, divided
• 1 teaspoon garlic powder, divided
• 1 cup buttermilk
• 1 tablespoon apple cider vinegar
• 1 tablespoon hot sauce
• ½ cup breadcrumbs
• Peanut oil, for frying
• 12 okras, cut into ½-inch slices
Preparation:
1. On a work surface, line up three small bowls. In the first bowl, stir together 1 cup of flour, ½ teaspoon of salt, ½ teaspoon of cayenne, and ½ teaspoon of garlic powder.
2. Whisk the buttermilk, vinegar, and hot sauce to combine in the second bowl.
3. In the third bowl, stir together the breadcrumbs and the remaining 1 cup of flour, ½ teaspoon of salt, ½ teaspoon of cayenne, and ½ teaspoon of garlic powder.
4. Heat 1 inch of oil to 375°F in a cast-iron skillet over high heat.
5. Dredge the okra slices in the seasoned flour, dip them in the buttermilk, and coat them in the seasoned bread crumbs.
6. Working in batches, fry the okra for 2 to 3 minutes per side, or until browned and crisp.

7. Transfer to a wire rack to cool slightly before serving.
Serving Suggestion: Serve with a spicy aioli dipping sauce.
Variation Tip: Omit cayenne for a milder taste.
Nutritional Information per Serving:
Calories 304 | Fat 7g | Sodium 584mg | Carbs 50.5g | Fiber 2.7g | Sugar 3.7g | Protein 8.8g

Roasted Artichokes with Fresh Lemon Juice

Prep Time: 10 minutes
Cook Time: 45 minutes
Serves: 4
Ingredients:
• 2 large artichokes, trimmed, halved, and chokes removed
• ¼ cup olive oil
• 4 garlic cloves, crushed
• Juice of 2 lemons, divided
• ½ teaspoon salt
Preparation:
1. Preheat the oven to 400°F.
2. Lay the artichokes in the skillet. Brush both sides with oil and arrange them, cut-side up, in a cast-iron skillet.
3. Fill the cavity of each artichoke half with one garlic clove. Flip the artichoke halves, cut-side down, taking care to keep the garlic nestled in the cavity.
4. Squeeze the juice of 1 lemon over the artichokes and sprinkle them with salt.
5. Roast the artichokes, uncovered, for 15 minutes. Cover the skillet with a lid or aluminum foil and bake for 25 to 30 minutes more, or until the artichokes are cooked through and tender.
6. Transfer the artichokes to a serving dish, and present them cut-side up, taking care to transfer the garlic with the artichokes.
7. Top with the remaining juice of 1 lemon and serve.
Serving Suggestion: Serve with aioli.
Variation Tip: For a spicier taste, add red pepper flakes.
Nutritional Information per Serving:
Calories 157 | Fat 12.8g | Sodium 368mg | Carbs 11.6g | Fiber 4.5g | Sugar 3.7g | Protein 2.9g

Fluffy Banana Cake

Prep Time: 15 minutes
Cook Time: 40 minutes
Serves: 12
Ingredients:
- ¾ cup white sugar
- 2 cups all-purpose flour
- 1 teaspoon baking soda
- 2 eggs
- 3 tablespoons sour cream
- 3 bananas, peeled and mashed
- ½ cup olive oil
- ½ cup walnuts

Preparation:
1. Preheat the oven to 350ºF and lightly grease a 12-inch cast-iron wok.
2. Add the flour, sugar, and baking soda to a bowl and mix well.
3. Add the egg, bananas, oil, and sour cream to another large-sized bowl and beat until well combined.
4. Merge in the flour mixture and mix until just combined.
5. Gently fold in the walnuts.
6. Place the mixture into the prepared wok.
7. Bake in the oven for about 40 minutes.
8. Remove the wok from the oven and place it onto a wire rack to cool for at least 15 minutes.
9. Carefully invert the cake onto the rack to cool completely.
10. Cut the cake into desired-sized slices and serve.

Serving Suggestion: Serve with a topping of whipped cream and banana slices.
Variation Tip: You can also use brown sugar instead of white sugar.
Nutritional Information per Serving:
Calories: 278|Fat: 13.8g|Sat Fat: 3.2g|Carbohydrates: 35.9g|Fiber: 1.7g|Sugar: 16.3g|Protein: 4.7g

Tasty Cherry Clafoutis

Prep Time: 15 minutes
Cook Time: 45 minutes
Serves: 8
Ingredients:
- ¾ cup whole milk
- 1 tablespoon unsalted butter, softened
- ½ cup heavy cream
- 2 tablespoons Amaretto
- ½ cup plus 2 tablespoons white sugar, divided
- ¼ teaspoon salt
- 3 tablespoons kirsch
- 4 large eggs
- ⅔ cup cake flour, sifted
- 3½ cups dark sweet cherries, pitted

Preparation:
1. Preheat the oven to 375ºF and generously grease a 10-inch cast-iron wok with butter.
2. Add the milk, cream, liqueurs, eggs, and ½ cup sugar to a blender and pulse well.
3. Fold in the flour and salt and pulse until well combined.
4. Put the mixture into a bowl and leave it for about 5 minutes.
5. Place ⅓ of the mixture into the prepared wok and bake in the oven for about 5 minutes.
6. Remove from the oven and top with the cherries, pressing them gently into the mixture.
7. Sprinkle the cherries with the remaining 2 tablespoons of sugar, followed by the remaining flour mixture.
8. Bake for about 45 minutes.
9. Remove the wok from the oven and place it onto a wire rack to cool slightly before slicing.

Serving Suggestion: Serve topped with fresh red cherries.
Variation Tip: You can also make clafoutis with other berries.
Nutritional Information per Serving:
Calories: 299|Fat: 7.7g|Sat Fat: 0.8g|Carbohydrates: 49.9g|Fiber: 2.7g|Sugar: 42.4g|Protein: 6.4g

Baked Cherry and Chocolate Cake

Prep Time: 10 minutes
Cook Time: 30 minutes
Serves: 6
Ingredients:
• ½ cup chocolate chips
• 1 can cherry pie filling
• 1½ cups lemon soda
• 1 box chocolate cake mix
Preparation:
1. Preheat the oven to 375°F.
2. Line a cast-iron Dutch oven with parchment paper.
3. Pour the pie filling into the prepared Dutch oven and spread evenly over the parchment paper.
4. Sprinkle the cake mix on top, then pour the soda over the cake mix.
5. Sprinkle the chocolate chips over the cake mix.
6. Bake in the preheated oven for 30 minutes.
Serving Suggestion: Remove from the oven and cool completely before serving.
Variation Tip: Add ½ teaspoon of vanilla essence.
Nutritional Information Per Serving:
Calories 567 | Fat 17g | Sodium 750mg | Carbs 100g | Fiber 3g | Sugar 40g | Protein 6g

Vanilla Cinnamon Pears

Prep Time: 10 minutes
Cook Time: 10 minutes
Serves: 4
Ingredients:

• 2 pounds pears, peeled, cored, and sliced
• ¼ teaspoon cinnamon
• ½ teaspoon ground ginger
• 2 tablespoons butter
• ½ cup orange juice
• ½ teaspoon vanilla
• 2 teaspoons fresh lemon juice
• 2 tablespoons sugar
• Pinch of salt
Preparation:
1. In a cast-iron skillet, add all the ingredients except the pears and cook over medium-high heat for 2 minutes.
2. Add the pears and bring to a boil.
3. Turn the heat to medium and cook until the sauce thickens, about 3–4 minutes.
Serving Suggestion: Allow to cool completely and serve.
Variation Tip: Add ¼ teaspoon of allspice.
Nutritional Information Per Serving:
Calories 222 | Fat 6g | Sodium 83mg | Carbs 44g | Fiber 7g | Sugar 30g | Protein 1.1g

Smooth Caramel Sauce

Prep Time: 10 minutes
Cook Time: 10 minutes
Serves: 2 cups
Ingredients:
• 1 cup granulated sugar
• ½ cup (1 stick) salted butter, cubed
• ½ cup heavy (whipping) cream
• 2 teaspoons vanilla extract
Preparation:
1. Melt the sugar in a cast-iron skillet over medium heat, constantly stirring with a wooden spoon. The sugar will clump and melt. Continue to stir as it turns amber brown, about 10 minutes.
2. Add the butter to the skillet and stir until fully melted and incorporated.
3. Remove the skillet from the heat and add the cream. Stir rapidly as the cream and sugar bubble and combine.
4. When thoroughly combined, the caramel sauce will be smooth and light brown.
5. Stir in the vanilla and let cool.
Serving Suggestion: Pour over grilled peaches, mix into turtle pies, or dip caramel apples into it.
Variation Tip: Add in chopped chocolate to make a chocolate caramel sauce.
Nutritional Information per Serving:
Calories 898 | Fat 57.1g | Sodium 339mg | Carbs 101.4g | Fiber 0g | Sugar 100.6g | Protein 1.1g

Baked Vanilla Cookie

Prep Time: 10 minutes
Cook Time: 15 minutes
Serves: 8
Ingredients:
- 1 egg
- 1 egg yolk
- 2 cups all-purpose flour
- ¾ teaspoon baking soda
- ¾ cup chocolate chips
- 1 teaspoon vanilla
- 1 cup brown sugar
- ½ cup butter, melted
- ¾ cup chocolate spread

Preparation:
1. Preheat the oven to 350°F.
2. Mix the egg yolk, egg, brown sugar, butter, vanilla, baking soda, and chocolate spread in a bowl until smooth.
3. Add the flour and stir until well combined.
4. Add the chocolate chips and fold well.
5. Pour the batter into a 10-inch cast-iron skillet and bake in the preheated oven for 15 minutes.

Serving Suggestion: Top with ice cream and serve.
Variation Tip: Add a pinch of salt.
Nutritional Information Per Serving:
Calories 385 | Fat 17g | Sodium 226mg | Carbs 51g | Fiber 1g | Sugar 25g | Protein 5g

Buttered Peach Cobbler

Prep Time: 10 minutes
Cook Time: 40 minutes
Serves: 12
Ingredients:
- ½ cup flour

- ¾ teaspoon cinnamon
- ¾ cup brown sugar
- 1¾ cups peaches, sliced
- ½ tablespoon baking powder
- ½ cup milk
- ¾ cup sugar
- 4 tablespoons butter

Preparation:
1. Preheat the oven to 375°F.
2. Melt the butter in a 10-inch cast-iron skillet over low heat.
3. Once the butter is melted, remove the skillet from the heat and set it aside.
4. Add the peaches and brown sugar to a saucepan and stir well. Bring to a boil over low heat until the sugar is melted.
5. Mix the flour, baking powder, sugar, and milk in a bowl and pour over the melted butter.
6. Once the peaches are ready, pour over the batter and sprinkle with the cinnamon.
7. Bake in the preheated oven for 40 minutes.

Serving Suggestion: Serve with whipping cream or ice cream.
Variation Tip: Add a pinch of salt.
Nutritional Information Per Serving:
Calories 149 | Fat 4g | Sodium 35mg | Carbs 28g | Fiber 0.6g | Sugar 23g | Protein 1g

Skillet-Cooked Cinnamon Apple Slices

Prep Time: 10 minutes
Cook Time: 15 minutes
Serves: 4
Ingredients:
- 6 gala apples, peeled, cored, and sliced
- 1 tablespoon apple cider vinegar
- ½ teaspoon cinnamon
- ½ cup brown sugar
- ¼ cup butter

Preparation:
1. Melt the butter in a 10-inch cast-iron skillet over medium heat.
2. Add the vinegar, cinnamon, and brown sugar and stir until the sugar is melted.
3. Add the apple slices, fold well, and cook for 10–15 minutes.

Serving Suggestion: Allow to cool completely, then serve.
Variation Tip: Add ¼ teaspoon of cardamom.
Nutritional Information Per Serving:
Calories 277 | Fat 12g | Sodium 87mg | Carbs 42g | Fiber 3g | Sugar 38g | Protein 0.5g

Coco Pudding Cake

Prep Time: 10 minutes
Cook Time: 35 minutes
Serves: 8
Ingredients:
• 1 cup flour
• 1¼ cups hot water
• 1 teaspoon vanilla extract
• ½ cup brown sugar
• ½ cup milk
• ⅓ cup butter, melted
• 2 teaspoons baking powder
• ½ cup cocoa powder
• 1¼ cups sugar
Preparation:
1. Preheat the oven to 350°F.
2. In a mixing bowl, mix the flour, ¾ cup of sugar, and ¼ cup of cocoa powder.
3. Add the butter, milk, and vanilla and beat until smooth.
4. Pour the batter into a greased 10-inch cast-iron skillet.
5. Mix the remaining sugar, cocoa powder, and brown sugar and sprinkle it over the batter.
6. Pour the hot water on top and bake in the preheated oven for 30–35 minutes.
Serving Suggestion: Serve with ice cream or whipped cream.
Variation Tip: Add a pinch of salt.
Nutritional Information Per Serving:
Calories 299 | Fat 8g | Sodium 68mg | Carbs 56g | Fiber 2g | Sugar 40g | Protein 3g

Homemade Apple Cake

Prep Time: 10 minutes
Cook Time: 60 minutes

Serves: 8
Ingredients:
• 1 box yellow cake mix
• 1 stick butter, cut into cubes
• 2 cans apple pie filling
Preparation:
1. Preheat the oven to 350°F.
2. Grease a cast-iron Dutch oven with cooking spray.
3. Pour the apple pie filling into the prepared Dutch oven.
4. Sprinkle the cake mix on top of the apple pie filling.
5. Spread the butter on top of the cake mix.
6. Bake in the preheated oven for 55–60 minutes.
Serving Suggestion: Serve with ice cream.
Variation Tip: Add ½ teaspoon of vanilla extract.
Nutritional Information Per Serving:
Calories 538 | Fat 19g | Sodium 584mg | Carbs 91g | Fiber 2g | Sugar 49g | Protein 3.2g

Palatable Peanut Butter Brownie

Prep Time: 10 minutes
Cook Time: 15 minutes
Serves: 2
Ingredients:
• 1 egg
• ½ cup peanut butter chips
• ¼ cup cocoa powder
• 6 tablespoons all-purpose flour
• 3 tablespoons canola oil
• 7 tablespoons sugar
• Pinch of salt
Preparation:
1. Preheat the oven to 350°F.
2. In a mixing bowl, whisk the eggs with the sugar until light.
3. Add the oil and stir well to combine.
4. Add the remaining ingredients and stir until just combined.
5. Pour the batter into a greased 8-inch cast-iron skillet and bake for 15 minutes.
Serving Suggestion: Let it cool completely, then slice and serve.
Variation Tip: Add 2 tablespoons of chocolate chips.
Nutritional Information Per Serving:
Calories 764 | Fat 40g | Sodium 151mg | Carbs 102g | Fiber 3.8g | Sugar 78g | Protein 7g

Wok-Cooked Caramelized Pineapple

Prep Time: 10 minutes
Cook Time: 16 minutes
Serves: 6
Ingredients:
• 1 fresh pineapple, peeled and cut into large slices
• ¼ cup butter
• ¼ cup brown sugar
• ¼ teaspoon ground cinnamon
Preparation:
1. Put the butter in a large-sized cast-iron wok and melt it over medium heat.
2. Place half of the pineapple slices in and sprinkle with some brown sugar.
3. Cook for about 4 minutes per side, basting with the butter occasionally.
4. Repeat for all the pineapple slices.
Serving Suggestion: Serve sprinkled with cinnamon.
Variation Tip: You can also make caramelized apricots with this recipe.
Nutritional Information per Serving:
Calories: 166|Fat: 7.9g|Sat Fat: 0.1g|Carbohydrates: 25.9g|Fiber: 2.2g|Sugar: 20.8g|Protein: 0.9g

Honey-Glazed Banana

Prep Time: 10 minutes
Cook Time: 8 minutes
Serves: 2
Ingredients:
• 1 tablespoon butter

• 2 ripe bananas, peeled and cut into ½-inch thick slices
• 2 tablespoons honey
• ⅛ teaspoon salt
• ½ teaspoon ground cinnamon
Preparation:
1. Heat the butter, honey, cinnamon, and salt over medium heat and stir to combine in a cast-iron wok.
2. Add the banana slices and cook for about 3 minutes per side until caramelized.
3. Serve warm.
Serving Suggestion: Serve with vanilla ice cream.
Variation Tip: You can replace honey with maple syrup.
Nutritional Information per Serving:
Calories: 221|Fat: 6.2g|Sat Fat: 0.9g|Carbohydrates: 44.7g|Fiber: 3.4g|Sugar: 31.7g|Protein: 1.4g

Pineapple Cherry Dump Cake with Almonds

Prep Time: 10 minutes
Cook Time: 60 minutes
Serves: 8
Ingredients:
• 1 box white cake mix
• 20-ounce can crushed pineapple
• 21-ounce can cherry pie filling
• ½ cup almonds, chopped
• 12 tablespoons butter, cut into pieces
Preparation:
1. Preheat the oven to 350°F.
2. Line a cast-iron Dutch oven with parchment paper.
3. Pour the cherry pie filling and crushed pineapple into the Dutch oven. Stir well.
4. Sprinkle the cake mix evenly over the mixture.
5. Sprinkle the almonds and butter over the cake mix.
6. Cover and bake in the preheated oven for 55–60 minutes.
Serving Suggestion: Allow to cool completely and serve.
Variation Tip: You can use your choice of chopped nuts instead of almonds.
Nutritional Information Per Serving:
Calories 589 | Fat 27g | Sodium 571mg | Carbs 82g | Fiber 1.8g | Sugar 43g | Protein 4.9g

Simple Baked Cake

Prep Time: 10 minutes
Cook Time: 35 minutes
Serves: 8
Ingredients:
• 2 cups sugar
• 2 cups self-rising flour
• 1¼ gallons milk
• 2 large eggs
• 1 tablespoon vanilla extract
• ¼ cup vegetable oil
• Powdered sugar, to serve
Preparation:
1. Preheat the oven to 350℉.
2. Use cooking spray and flour to coat a 12-inch cast-iron skillet.
3. Combine the flour, sugar, milk, eggs, vanilla, and oil in a mixing bowl until blended.
4. Pour the mixture into the skillet.
5. Bake for 35 minutes in the preheated oven.
6. Set aside the cake to cool.
7. Arrange on plates and serve.
Serving Suggestion: Sprinkle powdered sugar on top.
Variation Tip: Add a teaspoon of vanilla extract to make it a vanilla cake.
Nutritional Information per Serving:
Calories 400 | Fat 9.1g | Sodium 36mg | Carbs 75.9g | Fiber 0.8g | Sugar 52g | Protein 6.1g

Churros with Dipping Sauce

Prep Time: 10 minutes
Cook Time: 15 minutes
Serves: 3
Ingredients:
• 1 cup water
• ¾ stick butter
• 3 tablespoons granulated sugar
• 1 cup all-purpose flour
• ¼ teaspoon ground cinnamon
• ¼ teaspoon vanilla extract
• 3 eggs
• 1 cup peanut oil

For the topping:
• ½ cup sugar
• 1 tablespoon ground cinnamon
Preparation:
1. Combine the water, butter, and sugar in a medium saucepan over medium heat.
2. Add the flour, cinnamon, and vanilla, reduce the heat to low, and use a wooden spoon to stir vigorously until a ball of dough forms.
3. Remove from the heat and beat in the eggs, one at a time. Allow the dough to rest for a few minutes, then scoop it into a pastry bag fitted with a ½-inch star-shaped tip.
4. In a cast-iron skillet, heat the peanut oil over medium-high heat to 375°F.
5. Pipe the dough directly into the oil, cutting each churro off at 6 inches.
6. Fry for 2 minutes per side, transfer to a rack to cool and repeat with the remaining dough.
7. In a medium mixing bowl, combine the sugar and cinnamon. Roll the churros in the sugar and cinnamon when they're cool enough to handle.
8. Serve warm.
Serving Suggestion: Serve with a chocolate dipping sauce.
Variation Tip: Substitute peanut oil with vegetable oil.
Nutritional Information per Serving:
Calories 705 | Fat 45.7g | Sodium 228mg | Carbs 66.3g | Fiber 1.6g | Sugar 33.9g | Protein 10.1g

Vanilla Mango Cobbler

Prep Time: 10 minutes
Cook Time: 45 minutes
Serves: 2
Ingredients:
• 1½ cups mango, cubed
• ½ box vanilla cake mix
• ¼ cup water
• 1 tablespoon honey
• ½ tablespoon fresh ginger, grated
• 1 egg
• ½ teaspoon vanilla extract
• ½ tablespoon coconut oil
• ½ teaspoon allspice
• ½ tablespoon butter
Preparation:
1. Preheat the oven to 350℉.
2. In a bowl, combine the cake mix with the egg and the water and set aside.
3. Mix the mangoes, ginger, honey, butter, and allspice in another bowl.
4. Grease a cast-iron skillet with coconut oil.

5. Pour the mango mixture inside and add the cake mix, stirring gently to combine. Don't stir too much.
6. Bake in the oven for 35 to 40 minutes.
7. Cool and serve.

Serving Suggestion: Serve with ice cream.

Variation Tip: Substitute honey with maple syrup.

Nutritional Information per Serving:
Calories 276 | Fat 9.1g | Sodium 275mg | Carbs 47.3g | Fiber 2.8g | Sugar 35.9g | Protein 4g

Golden Rhubarb Cobbler

Prep Time: 15 minutes
Cook Time: 45 minutes
Serves: 8
Ingredients:
• ¾ cup light brown sugar
• ½ cup whole milk
• 4 cups rhubarb, chopped roughly
• 4 tablespoons butter, divided, melted, and cooled slightly
• 2 large eggs, lightly beaten
• 1½ cups all-purpose flour
• 1 cup granulated white sugar
• 1 teaspoon vanilla extract
• 2 teaspoons baking powder

Preparation:
1. Preheat the oven to 350°F and position a rack in the center of the oven.
2. Lightly grease a cast-iron frying pan.
3. Add the rhubarb and brown sugar to a large-sized bowl and toss to coat. Set aside.
4. Add 3 tablespoons of butter, eggs, milk, and vanilla to another medium-sized bowl and stir well.
5. Add the flour, baking powder, and sugar and with a thorough whisk, stir until the mixture becomes smooth.
6. Place the mixture into the prepared frying pan and spread evenly.
7. Place the rhubarb evenly over the mixture and pour over the remaining melted butter.

8. Bake for about 45 minutes until golden brown.

Serving Suggestion: Serve warm sprinkled with white sugar.

Variation Tip: Make sure to use unsalted butter.

Nutritional Information per Serving:
Calories: 319|Fat: 7.7g|Sat Fat: 1.1g|Carbohydrates: 59.5g|Fiber: 1.8g|Sugar: 38.6g|Protein: 5.1g

Chocolate and Peanut Cookie

Prep Time: 15 minutes
Cook Time: 18 minutes
Serves: 6
Ingredients:
• ⅓ cup unsweetened cocoa powder
• 1 cup all-purpose flour
• 1 teaspoon cornstarch
• ¼ teaspoon salt
• ½ cup butter
• ¼ cup brown sugar
• 1 cup peanut butter chips
• ½ teaspoon baking soda
• ½ cup white sugar
• 1 egg
• 1 teaspoon vanilla extract

Preparation:
1. Preheat the oven to 350ºF and generously grease a 9-inch cast-iron wok.
2. Combine the flour, cocoa powder, baking soda, cornstarch, and salt in a large-sized bowl and mix well.
3. In a medium-sized bowl, add the butter and sugars. Using an electric mixer, beat on medium speed until fluffy.
4. Add the eggs and vanilla extract and beat well.
5. Gently fold in the peanut butter chips.
6. Combine the wet and dry ingredients and put the mixture into the prepared wok.
7. Press the dough into an even layer, leaving a ½-inch border around the edges.
8. Bake in the oven for about 18 minutes until golden brown on top.
9. Remove from the oven and set it aside to cool for about 5 minutes before serving.

Serving Suggestions: Top with nuts.

Variation Tip: You can also use brown sugar.

Nutritional Information per Serving:
Calories: 535|Fat: 28.9g|Sat Fat: 8.9g|Carbohydrates: 63g|Fiber: 4.1g|Sugar: 38.8g|Protein: 12.2g

Caramelized Bananas with Cranberries

Prep Time: 10 minutes
Cook Time: 15 minutes
Serves: 2
Ingredients:
• 1½ tablespoons salted butter
• ½ cup loosely packed light brown sugar
• ⅛ cup water
• 2 firm yellow bananas, peeled and sliced
• ⅛ cup dried cranberries
• ⅛ cup toasted pumpkin seeds
Preparation:
1. Preheat a cast-iron skillet over low heat for 3 minutes.
2. Melt the butter in a bowl. Place the melted butter, brown sugar, and water in the pan and simmer for 3 to 5 minutes or until hot but not boiling.
3. Add the bananas and cook for 3 to 5 minutes or until the bananas soften. Remove from the heat.
4. Add the cranberries and seeds and gently stir until they're mixed in.
5. Serve and enjoy.
Serving Suggestion: Serve with ice cream.
Variation Tip: Substitute pumpkin seeds with sunflower seeds.
Nutritional Information per Serving:
Calories 387 | Fat 12.6g | Sodium 63mg | Carbs 72.2g | Fiber 3.6g | Sugar 59.4g | Protein 3.2g

Skillet-Fried Apples

Prep Time: 10 minutes
Cook Time: 25 minutes
Serves: 3
Ingredients:
• ½ cup (1 stick) salted butter
• ¼ cup packed brown sugar

• 2 tablespoons ground cinnamon
• 1 teaspoon ground allspice
• 1 teaspoon ground ginger
• 4 Granny Smith apples, skin left on, sliced ½-inch thick
Preparation:
1. In a cast-iron skillet over medium-high heat, melt the butter.
2. Sprinkle in the brown sugar, cinnamon, allspice, and ginger. Stir to combine.
3. Add the apples and stir to coat with the butter mixture. Cook, uncovered, for 3 to 4 minutes.
4. Reduce the heat to low and simmer, uncovered, for 15 to 20 minutes until the apples soften.
Serving Suggestion: Serve alongside biscuits, country ham, and scrambled eggs.
Variation Tip: Purée the apples for fried applesauce.
Nutritional Information per Serving:
Calories 487 | Fat 31.4g | Sodium 225mg | Carbs 57.5g | Fiber 9.8g | Sugar 42.8g | Protein 1.4g

Chocolate and Strawberry Pudding

Prep Time: 10 minutes
Cook Time: 45 minutes
Serves: 5
Ingredients:
• 1 tablespoon salted butter
• 1 loaf French bread, preferably day-old, broken into 1-inch pieces
• 1 cup chocolate chips
• 2 cups fresh strawberries, quartered
• 5 large eggs
• 2 cups whole milk
• 1 cup heavy (whipping) cream
• ½ cup sugar
• ¼ teaspoon ground ginger
• ¼ teaspoon vanilla extract
• 2 cups dehydrated strawberries, crushed (optional)
• Vanilla ice cream, for serving
Preparation:
1. Preheat the oven to 350°F.
2. Grease a cast-iron skillet with butter and evenly arrange the bread inside. Sprinkle with chocolate chips and fresh strawberries.
3. Whisk the eggs, milk, cream, sugar, ginger, and vanilla to combine in a large bowl. Evenly

pour the custard over the bread, being careful not to mix.

4. Top with an even layer of dehydrated strawberries (if using).

5. Bake for 45 minutes. Remove from the oven and cool, letting the filling set before serving.

Serving Suggestion: Serve with a scoop of vanilla ice cream.

Variation Tip: Substitute blackberries and white chocolate for the strawberries and chocolate chips.

Nutritional Information per Serving:
Calories 479 | Fat 22.9g | Sodium 186mg | Carbs 57.3g | Fiber 3.6g | Sugar 48.4g | Protein 13.1g

Yogurt Honey Cake

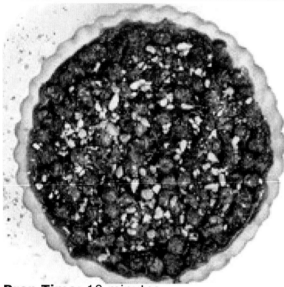

Prep Time: 10 minutes
Cook Time: 35 minutes
Serves: 8
Ingredients:
- 1 cup softened butter
- 5 tablespoons honey
- 2 large eggs
- ½ cup unsweetened yogurt
- 1 tablespoon vanilla extract
- 2 cups all-purpose flour
- 2 tablespoons baking soda
- ½ teaspoon salt

Toppings:
- Fresh fruit and honey
- Chopped pistachios

Preparation:
1. Preheat the oven to 350℉.
2. Lightly coat the inside of a 9-inch cast-iron skillet with cooking spray.
3. In a mixing dish, combine the butter and honey.
4. Stir in the eggs, vanilla extract, and yogurt until thoroughly combined.
5. Stir in ½ teaspoon of salt, two teaspoons of baking powder, and flour until smooth.
6. Pour the batter into the prepared skillet and bake in the preheated oven for 35 minutes.
7. Remove the cake from the oven and place it on a serving platter to cool.
8. Place the fruit, honey, and pistachios on top of the cake.

9. Cut into slices before serving.

Serving Suggestion: Serve with a hot beverage.

Variation Tip: Feel free to use a sweetener of your choice.

Nutritional Information per Serving:
Calories 376 | Fat 13.3g | Sodium 261mg | Carbs 60.6g | Fiber 1g | Sugar 36.1g | Protein 5.9g

Sweet Apple Pie

Prep Time: 10 minutes
Cook Time: 1 hour and 22 minutes
Serves: 6
Ingredients:
- 2 pounds' apple, peeled, cored, and diced
- 1 teaspoon ground cinnamon
- ¾ pound granulated sugar
- ½ pound butter, melted
- 1-pound brown sugar
- 2 pie crusts
- 1 egg white, beaten
- 2 tablespoons white sugar

Preparation:
1. Preheat the oven to 350℉ and position an oven rack in the middle of the oven.
2. Melt the butter in a medium-sized pot, stir in the brown sugar and simmer for 2 minutes before transferring it to a bowl.
3. Combine the diced apples, butter mixture, granulated sugar, and cinnamon in a mixing dish.
4. Grease a 10-inch cast-iron skillet and place one pie crust in it.
5. Spread the apple mixture over the pie crust and top with the second pie crust.
6. Seal the filling by pressing or crimping the edges. In a mixing dish, whisk together an egg white and a tablespoon of water.
7. Use an egg wash to brush the top of the apple pie.
8. Sprinkle with two tablespoons of sugar and make four slits on the top.
9. Bake for 1 hour and 10 minutes or until the apple pie is golden brown.
10. Allow the pie to cool before serving.

Serving Suggestion: Serve with ice cream.

Variation Tip: You can also use homemade pie crusts.

Nutritional Information per Serving:
Calories 298 | Fat 15.5g | Sodium 115mg | Carbs 42.7g | Fiber 3.5g | Sugar 38.5g | Protein 1g

Blackberries and Raspberries Cobbler

Prep Time: 10 minutes
Cook Time: 40 minutes
Serves: 6
Ingredients:
- 2 cups fresh blackberries
- 2 cups fresh raspberries
- 1 cup granulated sugar
- ½ cup all-purpose flour
- 1 teaspoon corn starch
- ¼ teaspoon salt
- 1 cup all-purpose unbleached flour
- ¾ pound rolled oats
- ½ cup sugar
- ½ teaspoon salt
- ½ teaspoon cinnamon
- 1½ cold, unsalted sticks (¾ cup) butter, cut into tiny cubes

Preparation:
1. Preheat the oven to 375℉.
2. In a 10-inch cast-iron pan, combine the corn starch, salt, ½ cup of flour, sugar, and berries.
3. In the bowl of a stand mixer, combine the 1 cup of flour, oats, cinnamon, sugar, and salt.
4. Stir in the butter until it's equally distributed. Spread the oat mixture on top of the berry mixture.
5. Bake the cobbler in a preheated oven for 40 minutes.
6. Arrange on plates and serve warm.
Serving Suggestion: Serve with berry puree.
Variation Tip: Feel free to use any other berries of your choice.
Nutritional Information per Serving:
Calories 472 | Fat 19.8g | Sodium 370mg | Carbs 70.7g | Fiber 3.6g | Sugar 25.1g | Protein 6.5g

Tasty Blueberry Cake

Prep Time: 15 minutes
Cook Time: 25 minutes
Serves: 8
Ingredients:
- 1 cup whole milk
- 3 large eggs
- ½ cup white whole-wheat flour
- ¼ teaspoon salt
- 2 tablespoons butter, melted
- ¼ cup plus 1 tablespoon white sugar, divided
- ½ teaspoon vanilla extract
- 2½ cups blueberries, frozen

Preparation:
1. Preheat the oven to 400°F and lightly grease a 9-inch cast-iron wok.
2. In a blender, add the eggs, flour, milk, ¼ cup of sugar, salt, and vanilla extract; pulse until smooth.
3. Add the butter and pulse for about 30 seconds more.
4. Evenly place the blueberries in the bottom of the prepared wok and top with the flour mixture.
5. Dust evenly with the remaining sugar.
6. Bake for about 25 minutes and serve warm.
Serving Suggestion: Serve with a drizzle of blueberry syrup.
Variation Tip: You can also use fresh blueberries.
Nutritional Information per Serving:
Calories: 150|Fat: 6g|Sat Fat: 0.8g|Carbohydrates: 20.9g|Fiber: 1.8g|Sugar: 14g|Protein: 4.7g

Pecan Brownie Pie

Prep Time: 15 minutes
Cook Time: 30 minutes
Serves: 6
Ingredients:
- ⅓ cup cocoa powder
- ½ cup all-purpose flour
- ¼ teaspoon salt
- ½ cup butter, melted
- 1 teaspoon vanilla extract
- 1 cup white sugar
- 2 large eggs
- ½ cup pecans, chopped

Preparation:
1. Preheat the oven to 350ºF and lightly grease a 9-inch cast-iron wok.
2. In a bowl, mix the flour, cocoa powder, and salt.
3. In another large-sized bowl, add the sugar and butter and beat well.
4. Blend in the eggs and vanilla and beat well.
5. Add the flour mixture to the wet mixture and mix until well combined.
6. Gently fold in the pecans.
7. Evenly place the mixture into the prepared wok.
8. Bake in the oven for about 30 minutes.
9. Serve warm.

Serving Suggestion: Serve with vanilla ice cream.
Variation Tip: You can use walnuts instead of pecans.
Nutritional Information per Serving:
Calories: 407|Fat: 25.1g|Sat Fat: 4.3g|Carbohydrates: 45.6g|Fiber: 3g|Sugar: 34g|Protein: 5.4g

Butter Gingerbread Cake

Prep Time: 15 minutes
Cook Time: 40 minutes
Serves: 8
Ingredients:
- ½ cup white sugar
- 2 cups all-purpose flour
- 2 teaspoons ground ginger
- 1 teaspoon baking soda
- ½ cup salted butter, melted
- 1 large egg, beaten
- 1 teaspoon ground cinnamon
- ⅔ cup molasses
- 1⅓ cups buttermilk

Preparation:
1. Preheat the oven to 350ºF and grease a 10-inch cast-iron wok.
2. Combine the flour, sugar, spices, and baking soda in a bowl.
3. In another large-sized bowl, add the molasses and butter and beat well.
4. Add the buttermilk and egg and beat until well combined.
5. Add the flour mixture and mix well.
6. Place the mixture into the prepared wok.
7. Bake in the oven for about 40 minutes.
8. Remove the wok from the oven and place it onto a wire rack to cool for at least 15 minutes before slicing.

Serving Suggestion: Serve with a topping of whipped cream.
Variation Tip: You can also use brown sugar instead of white sugar.
Nutritional Information per Serving:
Calories: 369|Fat: 12.9g|Sat Fat: 3.4g|Carbohydrates: 59.3g|Fiber: 1.1g|Sugar: 29.8g|Protein: 5.5g

4-Week Meal Plan

Week-1

Day-1
Breakfast: Cheesy Omelet
Lunch: Bow-Tie Pasta with Asparagus
Snack: Tasty White Bean Chili
Dinner: Palatable Tuna Patties
Dessert: Honey-Glazed Banana

Day-2
Breakfast: Baked Butter Cornbread
Lunch: Butter Shrimp with Red Pepper Flakes
Snack: Baked Yukon Gold Potatoes
Dinner: Basil Chicken Thighs
Dessert: Tasty Cherry Clafoutis

Day-3
Breakfast: Eggs in Bell Pepper
Lunch: Wok-Fried Mushroom with Spinach and Scallion
Snack: Fried Flour-Coated Okra
Dinner: Chicken Stew with Gumbo
Dessert: Butter Gingerbread Cake

Day-4
Breakfast: Peanut Butter Oatmeal
Lunch: Sautéed Spicy Shrimp
Snack: Garlic Chicken Thighs
Dinner: Bacon and Bean Stew in Chicken Broth
Dessert: Simple Baked Cake

Day-5
Breakfast: Fried Eggs and Bacon
Lunch: Roasted Cabbage Strips
Snack: Baked Marinated Beans
Dinner: Onion and Fish Stew
Dessert: Baked Cherry and Chocolate Cake

Day-6
Breakfast: Scrambled Tomato and Pepper
Lunch: Baked Penne Pasta
Snack: Light Fried Broccoli
Dinner: Spicy Butter-Fried Salmon
Dessert: Pecan Brownie Pie

Day-7
Breakfast: Fluffy Milk Cornbread
Lunch: Delectable Veggie Fajitas
Snack: Parmesan Turkey Meatballs
Dinner: Simple Juicy Mignon Steak
Dessert: Pineapple Cherry Dump Cake with Almonds

Week-2

Day-1
Breakfast: Green Apple Omelet
Lunch: Chicken Pasta with Tomato Sauce
Snack: Creamy Tomato and Carrot Soup
Dinner: Thyme Scallops
Dessert: Fluffy Banana Cake

Day-2
Breakfast: Tasty Oat Pancakes
Lunch: Spicy Cod Fillets
Snack: Coconut Mushroom Soup
Dinner: Rosemary Chicken Thighs
Dessert: Vanilla Cinnamon Pears

Day-3
Breakfast: Scrambled Potatoes with Mushrooms
Lunch: Creamy Pumpkin Pasta
Snack: Ground Turkey, Onion and Potato Soup
Dinner: Honey Pork Chops
Dessert: Churros with Dipping Sauce

Day-4
Breakfast: Crispy Sweet Potatoes
Lunch: Baked Chicken Thighs
Snack: Bacon Bean Soup
Dinner: Delectable Pork Tenderloin Pieces
Dessert: Vanilla Mango Cobbler

Day-5
Breakfast: Baked Cheese Bread
Lunch: Roasted Vegetable Mixture
Snack: Carrot and Yellow Onion Soup
Dinner: Roast Beef Tenderloin with Horseradish Sauce
Dessert: Skillet-Cooked Cinnamon Apple Slices

Day-6
Breakfast: Butter Chicken Asparagus Frittata
Lunch: Creamy Chicken Thighs
Snack: Garlicky Green Beans
Dinner: Curry Beef with Veggie
Dessert: Palatable Peanut Butter Brownie

Day-7
Breakfast: Bacon and Asparagus Frittata
Lunch: Cauliflower Steaks with Butter Mixture
Snack: Parmesan Asparagus
Dinner: Beef and Bean Casserole
Dessert: Baked Vanilla Cookie

Week-3

Day-1
Breakfast: Skillet-Fried Sweet Potatoes
Lunch: Spicy Ramen Noodles
Snack: Fried Flour-Coated Okra
Dinner: Palatable Juicy Pork Tenderloin
Dessert: Coco Pudding Cake

Day-2
Breakfast: Tater Tot Sausage Pizza
Lunch: Onion Turkey Burgers
Snack: Garlicky Green Beans
Dinner: Thyme Duck Breast Slices
Dessert: Golden Rhubarb Cobbler

Day-3
Breakfast: Vanilla Dates and Quinoa
Lunch: Garlic Chicken Thighs with Mushroom
Snack: Wok-Cooked Broccoli and Cauliflower
Dinner: Juicy Pork Chops with Onion and Apple
Dessert: Palatable Peanut Butter Brownie

Day-4
Breakfast: Turkey and Veggies Hash
Lunch: Baked Chicken and Potato with Parsley
Snack: Carrot and Onion Soup
Dinner: Walnut Pasta with Mushroom Sauce
Dessert: Chocolate and Peanut Cookie

Day-5
Breakfast: Chicken Zucchini Pancakes with Scallion
Lunch: Spaghetti Carbonara
Snack: Garlicky Green Beans
Dinner: Seared Lobster Tails with Parsley
Dessert: Chocolate and Strawberry Pudding

Day-6
Breakfast: Scalloped Potatoes
Lunch: Honey Mustard Salmon Fillets
Snack: Roasted Artichokes with Fresh Lemon Juice
Dinner: Herbed Lamb Chops with Salted Butter
Dessert: Yogurt Honey Cake

Day-7
Breakfast: Simple Caprese Eggs
Lunch: Roasted Baby Potatoes
Snack: Kale, Bean, and Potato Stew in Vegetable Soup
Dinner: Beef Stew with Tomatoes
Dessert: Sweet Apple Pie

Week-4

Day-1
Breakfast: Onion and Sweet Potato Frittata
Lunch: Sautéed Rice Noodles with Snow Peas
Snack: Brussels Sprouts Casserole with Cheeses
Dinner: Delicious Beef Bourguignon
Dessert: Caramelized Bananas with Cranberries

Day-2
Breakfast: Chees Tomato Frittata
Lunch: Chili Chickpeas Stew with Carrot
Snack: Wok-Cooked Broccoli and Cauliflower
Dinner: Roasted Chicken with Leeks
Dessert: Blackberries and Raspberries Cobbler

Day-3
Breakfast: Vanilla Oatmeal
Lunch: Cheesy Penne Pasta with Sausage
Snack: Hearty Chili Beans and Tomato Stew
Dinner: Lemony Pork Chops
Dessert: Skillet-Fried Apples

Day-4
Breakfast: Garlic Cheese Waffles
Lunch: Tomato and Chicken Pasta
Snack: Zucchini and Ripe Tomato Gratin
Dinner: Lemon Honey Salmon
Dessert: Tasty Blueberry Cake

Day-5
Breakfast: Sausage and Potato Hash
Lunch: Honey Sriracha Brussels Sprouts
Snack: Garlicky Green Beans
Dinner: Herbed Rib-eye Steak
Dessert: Homemade Apple Cake

Day-6
Breakfast: Cheese Orange Pancakes
Lunch: Grilled Salmon
Snack: Spicy Quinoa
Dinner: Lemony Turkey Breast
Dessert: Buttered Peach Cobbler

Day-7
Breakfast: Flavorful Shakshuka
Lunch: Scrambled Ground Beef with Mushrooms
Snack: Parmesan Asparagus
Dinner: Delicious Fried Strip Steak
Dessert: Wok-Cooked Caramelized Pineapple

Conclusion

Cooking in the Cast Iron Cookware is fun and enhances the great taste of your food. It is the old method of cooking but effective through. You can cook whatever you want and the Cast Iron Cookware will be your all-in-one cooking tool. It will be your cooking pot, your baking oven as well as your baking tray. With little care, you can manage your pot and with the help of this cookbook, you will be able to cook amazing delicious recipes of all time. You can cook your steaks, soups, and sauces as well as bake your tarts, skillet cookies in it. You can prepare your breakfast at the camp site like a pro as it is not affected by heat.

You can cook whatever you want and this guide will help you to manage your pot and cooking and you will be praised for your cooking skills. With the help of this book, you can maintain your Cast Iron Cookware effectively and cook delicious food like an expert. So guy, let's get started to create new masterpieces with help of this book and amazing Cast Iron Cookware.

Appendix 1 Measurement Conversion Chart

WEIGHT EQUIVALENTS

US STANDARD	METRIC (APPROXINATE)
1 ounce	28 g
2 ounces	57 g
5 ounces	142 g
10 ounces	284 g
15 ounces	425 g
16 ounces (1 pound)	455 g
1.5pounds	680 g
2pounds	907 g

VOLUME EQUIVALENTS (DRY)

US STANDARD	METRIC (APPROXIMATE)
⅛ teaspoon	0.5 mL
¼ teaspoon	1 mL
½ teaspoon	2 mL
¾ teaspoon	4 mL
1 teaspoon	5 mL
1 tablespoon	15 mL
¼ cup	59 mL
½ cup	118 mL
¾ cup	177 mL
1 cup	235 mL
2 cups	475 mL
3 cups	700 mL
4 cups	1 L

TEMPERATURES EQUIVALENTS

FAHRENHEIT(F)	CELSIUS (C) (APPROXIMATE)
225 °F	107 °C
250 °F	120 °C
275 °F	135 °C
300 °F	150 °C
325 °F	160 °C
350 °F	180 °C
375 °F	190 °C
400 °F	205 °C
425 °F	220 °C
450 °F	235 °C
475 °F	245 °C
500 °F	260 °C

VOLUME EQUIVALENTS (LIQUID)

US STANDARD	US STANDARD (OUNCES)	METRIC (APPROXIMATE)
2 tablespoons	1 fl.oz	30 mL
¼ cup	2 fl.oz	60 mL
½ cup	4 fl.oz	120 mL
1 cup	8 fl.oz	240 mL
1½ cup	12 fl.oz	355 mL
2 cups or 1 pint	16 fl.oz	475 mL
4 cups or 1 quart	32 fl.oz	1 L
1 gallon	128 fl.oz	4 L

Made in United States
North Haven, CT
02 June 2023

37279576R00069